The **RYA**

Inter

Certificate of

Competence

Other titles in the RYA series from Adlard Coles Nautical

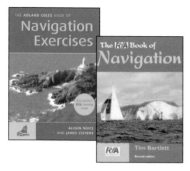

The RYA Book of Navigation 2nd edition by Tim Barlett ISBN 0-7136-6322-7

This is the reference text for anyone following RYA navigation courses from Day Skipper through to Yachtmaster Offshore. By the end of the book readers should be fully conversant with what it takes to navigate a yacht or motorboat from one port to another safely and accurately.

The Adlard Coles Book of Navigation Exercises by Alison Noice and James Stevens ISBN 0-7136-6323-5

A companion to the bestselling manual *The RYA Book of Navigation*, providing practice questions and answers at both Day Skipper and Coast Skipper/Yachtmaster level. An invaluable back-up to anyone attending RYA shorebased courses and those wishing to brush up on their knowledge of navigation and seamanship.

The RYA Book of Diesel Engines 2nd edition by Tim Bartlett ISBN 0-7136-6358-8

Based on the RYA's one-day diesel engine course, this book explains how a diesel engine works and how to look after it, and is aimed at boatowners rather than experienced mechanics. A must for anyone who puts to sea with a diesel-powered boat.

The RYA Book of Outboard Motors 2nd edition by Tim Bartlett ISBN 0-7136-6873-3

Aimed at boatowners rather than experienced mechanics, this book explains how an outboard motor works and how to look after it. Covers both two-stroke and four-stroke engines.

The Adlard Coles Book of EuroRegs for Inland Waterways 2nd edition by Marian Martin ISBN 0-7136-6589-0

Written especially for pleasure craft, this book is essential for anyone travelling on the inland waterways of Europe. Covers signs, signals, flags, lights, buoyage, landmarks, procedures in tunnels, locks and weirs, and overtaking rules.

Available through bookshops, chandlers and the Adlard Coles website www.adlardcoles.com. In case of difficulty, contact: MDL Distribution Ltd, Brunel Road, Houndsmill, Basingstoke RG21 6XS; tel: 01256 302692; fax: 01256 812 558/521; email: mdl@macmillan.co.uk

The **RYA** Book of the

International Certificate of Competence

Bill Anderson

Adlard Coles Nautical
London

Published by Adlard Coles Nautical
an imprint of A & C Black Publishers Ltd
37 Soho Square, London W1D 3QZ
www.adlardcoles.com

First edition published 2002
Reprinted 2003, 2004

ISBN-10: 0-7136-6248-4
ISBN-13: 978-0-7136-6248-1

A CIP catalogue record for this book is available from the
British Library.

A & C Black uses paper produced with elemental chlorine-free
pulp, harvested from managed sustainable forests

Typeset in 10 on 12pt Concorde
Printed and bound in Singapore by Tien Wah Press Limited

Note: While all reasonable care has been taken in the
publication of this book, the publisher takes no responsibility
for the use of the methods or products described in the book.

Acknowledgements
The author and publisher wish to thank the following
organisations for their assistance in the illustration of this book:

Yachting Monthly
Macmillan Nautical Almanac
The Hydrographer of the Navy for permission to use extracts
from the British Admiralty RYA Training Chart 1

Contents

Introduction ix

Eligibility x
Categories of ICC x

Exemptions from the ICC test . . xii
Applying to take the ICC test . . xii

The Written Test 1

The syllabus 1

A All Candidates: Regulations . 2

1 Knows responsibility for
keeping a proper lookout 2
2 Can determine a 'safe speed' . . 2
3 Can recognise a potential
collision situation 2
4 Can identify 'give-way' vessel
in a collision situation 3
5 Knows what action to take as
'give-way' and 'stand-on' vessel . 4
6 Knows the responsibilities of a
small vessel in a narrow
channel 6
7 Can recognise manoeuvring
signals (1,2,3, and 5 short
blasts) 6
8 Can make and recognise visual
distress signals 6

Self-test Questions on Regulations 7

A All Candidates: Safety 9

1 Is able to use and instruct crew
on the use of lifejackets;
distress flares; fire extinguishers;
kill cord (if fitted) 9
Lifejackets 9
Distress flares: red rocket
parachute flares; red hand
flares; orange smoke signals . . 10
Fire extinguishers 10
The kill cord 11
2 Can prepare a boat for use and
take sensible precautions before
setting out, including: engine
checks; check fuel for range/
duration of trip; obtain weather
forecast; avoid overloading boat . 11
Engine checks 11
Fuel and operating range or
duration 12
Obtaining weather forecasts . 12
Avoiding overloading the boat 13

Self-test Questions on Safety . . . 14

B Inland Only: CEVNI (European Code for Inland Waterways) . 15

Rules of the Road 15
Lights and day shapes 16
Waterway signs 17
Marking 19

Self-test Questions on CEVNI . . 20

C Candidates for Coastal Waters: Regulations 22

1 Knows the rules relating to Traffic Separation Schemes 22
2 Knows the requirements for navigation lights and shapes to be displayed by own vessel 23
3 Can recognise the following from their lights: power driven and sailing vessel; vessel at anchor; tug and tow; dredger . . 24
4 Knows sound signals to be made by vessels in Section 3 above . . 27

Self-test Questions for Coastal Waters: Regulations 28

C Candidates for Coastal Waters: Pilotage 30

1 Can recognise, by day and night, and understand the significance of buoys of the IALA system . . 30
 Cardinal buoys 30
 Lateral buoys 31

2 Knows sources of information on: local regulations; port entry and departure signals; VTS and Port Operations Radio 33
3 Can plan a harbour entry/departure, taking account of possible presence of large vessels and avoiding navigational hazards 33

Self-test Questions for Coastal Waters: Pilotage 35

C Candidates for Coastal Waters: Navigation 36

1 Can interpret a navigational chart, understand the significance of charted depths and drying heights and identify charted hazards . . 36
2 Can plot position by cross bearings and by latitude and longitude 38
3 Can determine magnetic course to steer, making allowance for leeway and tidal stream 38
4 Can use a tide table to find times and heights of high and low water at a standard port 41
5 Can determine direction and rate of tidal stream from a tidal stream atlas or tidal diamonds on a chart 42

Self-test Questions for Coastal Waters: Navigation 44

The Practical Test ·························· **47**

1 *Start:* Give safety briefing including use of safety equipment; has listened to weather forecasts; pre-start engine checks; start engine; check cooling; know fuel range 47

2 *Depart from pontoon:* understand use of springs to depart from lee wall/pontoon; communicate with crew; position fenders correctly 47

3 *360° turn in confined space* ... 49

4 *Securing to buoy:* communicate effectively with crew; prepare warp; choose correct angle of approach; control speed of approach; secure boat effectively; depart from the mooring safely 50

5 *Man overboard:* observe MOB or instruct crew to do so; demonstrate correct direction and speed of approach; make suitable contact with MOB 52

6a *High speed manoeuvres (if appropriate);* use kill cord if appropriate; choose suitable area; show awareness of other water users; warn crew before each

manoeuvre; look round before S and U turns; control speed on U turns; emergency stop ... 53

6b *Handling under sail (if appropriate):* sail a triangular course with one leg to windward; choose suitable area for hoisting/ lowering sails; use sails suitable for prevailing conditions; show awareness of wind direction; trim sails correctly on each point of sailing; warn crew before making manoeuvres; look round before tacking and gybing; control sails during tacking and gybing 53

7 *Coming alongside windward pontoon:* communicate effectively with crew; show awareness of other water users; prepare warps/fenders; choose correct angle of approach; control speed of approach; stop boat in place required and secure to pontoon; stop engine 54

Self-test Answers 57

Index 65

Introduction

The International Certificate of Competence, ICC for short, is an invention of the United Nations Economic Commission for Europe, Inland Transport Committee, Working Part on Inland Water Transport. Its purpose is to provide boatowners and charterers with a document issued in their own country and recognised throughout Europe. The agreement which sets up the rules for the issue of certificates is titled International Certificate for Operators of Pleasure Craft, Resolution No 40.

The rules on where, and for what type of boat, you might need to have a certificate as a visitor vary from country to country. In some you will need a certificate on inland but not in coastal waters and you may need a certificate only for motorboats, or for boats over a particular length, capable of a speed in excess of a certain number of knots or with engines over a certain power. Individual countries change their rules from time to time and the actual practice of local maritime officials has been reported as being at variance with national regulations. In some countries, whose laws require certificates for all boat users, the local harbour masters and marine police are not in the least interested, while in others, whose laws do not require visitors to have certificates, harbour masters ask to see them and there is much tut-tutting if one cannot be produced.

As a general rule, the further inland and the further south you go, the more likely it is that you will need to carry a Certificate of Competence. Many applicants for certificates take the view that, even though they may not strictly have to have one, it is easier to take the test in English than to waste a day's holiday on a multilingual argument with a harbour master or immigration official who is insisting that a certificate must be produced before the entry or exit formalities can be completed.

ICCs are issued in the UK by the Royal Yachting Association and by the British Water Ski Federation. This book covers the test which anyone applying to the RYA for a certificate needs to be able to pass. It is not intended to be a complete textbook on everything you need to know to pass the ICC, because it is assumed that if you are a boatowner you already have a degree of knowledge and competence. However, we all have gaps in our knowledge so we are nervous about taking tests. This book provides a revision guide for boatowners who need to take the ICC test and can do so with complete confidence.

Eligibility

Any country which issues ICCs may do so only for its own nationals or residents. Quite how long this condition can survive European Union legislation is open to doubt, but that is the way it stands at present. The RYA takes a pragmatic approach to the residency condition for applicants who are not British Nationals. If they can produce evidence of paying community charge, rent for a long-term leased property, are in full time employment in the UK, or are married to and living at the same UK address as a British national, then they can apply to the RYA for a certificate.

The minimum age for the issue of a certificate is 16 and applicants must, to quote from the Resolution, 'be physically and mentally fit and in particular must have sufficient powers of vision and hearing'. No specific medical or test of sanity is required; the competence test contains a practical element, which you would not be able to pass if you were not physically fit to skipper a boat.

Categories of ICC

ICCs can be valid for:
- Inland or coastal waters
- Power craft or sailing craft
- Both categories of water
- Both power and sail.

The test which you have to take is dictated by the categories of water and boat that you wish to use. Resolution No 40 offers no definition of motorboat or sailing boat so you simply have to use your common sense in deciding where the dividing line between a motorsailer, for which a certificate valid for power and sail is appropriate, and a motorboat with steadying sails lies (Fig 1). Inland waters are generally taken to be anything inland of a lock but not including locked basins which do not provide access to an inland waterways transport system.

There is a major difference between the tests for inland and coastal ICCs which makes the inland version difficult for Brits. The European inland waterways system is on a totally different scale to our narrow canals. It is used as a serious transport system with large barges carrying hundreds of tons of cargo. The rules for conduct on mainland European waterways are based on the Code Européen des Voies de la Navigation Interieure, commonly known as CEVNI. If you want an ICC valid for inland waters you have to show that you have a knowledge of CEVNI.

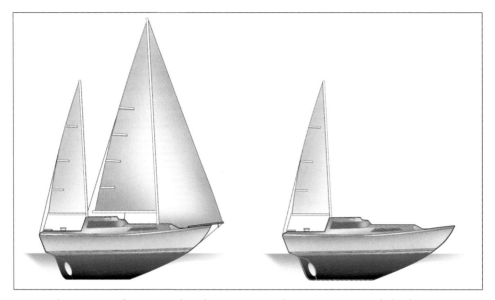

Fig 1 *This motorsailer is a sailing boat. Remove her mainmast and she becomes a motorboat with a steadying sail*

This is not as difficult as it may seem, because while CEVNI has some dauntingly complicated rules, it shares the basic right-of-way rules with the International Regulations for Preventing Collisions at Sea.

There is no special category of ICC for personal watercraft. If you intend to take a personal watercraft on holiday to a country which requires Certificates of Competence you have two options. You can take the RYA personal watercraft course and gain the certificate; although this is not a certificate with any specific international standing, the RYA will provide you with a short statement, in all the major European languages, explaining that your certificate is evidence of completing a course in the

safe handling of personal watercraft. Alternatively, you could take the ICC test in a small motorboat, and while some of it is not particularly relevant to personal watercraft, it will provide you with an internationally recognised certificate.

ICCs issued by the RYA are valid for boats up to 24m in length. This does not mean that you have to be capable of handling a 24m boat in order to take the test; you can take it in your own 4m outboard runabout. But just as you need no national certificate to use a pleasure craft up to 24m in length in the UK, it is assumed that you will have the good sense not to move up to a much larger boat without taking some expert advice and instruction.

COURSE COMPLETION CERT OR CERT OF COMPETENCE HELD	ICC MAY BE ISSUED FOR:			
	Power	Sail	Inland (CEVNI test required)	Coastal waters
National Powerboat Cert (Non Tidal) Level 2 or above	Yes	No	Yes	No
National Powerboat Cert (Tidal) Level 2 or above	Yes	No	Yes	Yes
Helmsman's Course Completion Cert	Yes	No	Yes	No
Inland – Helmsman Cert	Yes	No	Yes	No
Day Skipper Practical Course Completion Cert (Power)	Yes	No	Yes	Yes
Day Skipper Practical Course Completion Cert (Sail)	Yes	Yes	Yes	Yes
Coastal Skipper Practical Course Completion Cert (Power)	Yes	No	Yes	Yes
Coastal Skipper Practical Course Completion Cert (Sail)	Yes	Yes	Yes	Yes
Coastal Skipper (or higher) RYA/DoT Cert of Competence (Power)	Yes	No	Yes	Yes
Coastal Skipper (or higher) RYA/DoT Cert of Competence (Sail)	Yes	Yes	Yes	Yes
DoT Deck Officer Cert of Competence (Any Grade)	Yes	No	Yes	Yes
RN, Army or RAF Bridge Watchkeeping Cert	Yes	No	Yes	Yes
DoT or Local Authority Boatman's Licence	Yes	No	Yes	Yes
DoT Boatmaster Cert	Yes	No	No	No
RYA Dinghy Instructor or Dinghy level 5 and Powerboat L2	Yes	Yes	Yes	Yes

Exemptions from the ICC test

You do not have to take a test for the ICC if you already hold a Certificate of Competence or an RYA practical course completion certificate for skippering the type of boat in the category of water for which you want an ICC. The most commonly held certificates that entitle the holder to the issue of an ICC without taking an additional test are shown above.

If you hold a certificate that is not on this list, but you believe is of an equivalent or higher standard, you should consult the RYA to see if it can be accepted. For details of the CEVNI test, see the inland waters section on page 15.

Applying to take the ICC test

Tests are carried out by most RYA Recognised teaching establishments in the type of boats and in the categories of water for which they hold RYA recognition to teach. Tests are also available at some RYA affiliated clubs which have suitably qualified testers. A full list of centres is available from the RYA.

The Written Test

The syllabus

The syllabus for the written test is divided into three sections:

A This section applies to all candidates and includes a basic knowledge of the International Regulations for Preventing Collisions at Sea and safety.

B This section applies only to candidates for certificates valid for inland waterways. It covers the European Code for Inland Waterways (CEVNI).

C This section applies only to candidates for certificates valid for coastal waters. It includes a more detailed knowledge of the International Regulations for Preventing Collisions at Sea, pilotage and navigation.

The written test does not differentiate between certificates valid for power or sail.

If you wish to claim exemption from the test because you hold an RYA Certificate of Competence or practical course completion certificate and you want a certificate valid for inland waters, you will have to take just section B of the written test.

The syllabus for the written test is quite brief. The text in bold is the actual syllabus, all the rest is a description of what you have to know and self-test questions.

All Candidates: Regulations

This section is about the International Regulations for Preventing Collisions at Sea. You don't need to be able to quote from the rules, neither do you have to know which rule number says what. You just have to know what the most important rules mean, in practical terms, to the skipper of a small boat.

- At night, background lights ashore which may make it difficult to pick out the navigation lights of ships and other boats
- Weather and sea conditions
- The width of the channel in which you are navigating and the depth of water

1 Knows responsibility for keeping a proper lookout

You must keep a good lookout all the time, by sight and hearing and also by radar if you have it.

2 Can determine a 'safe speed'

You must not go so fast that your speed makes it impossible for you to spot approaching vessels or to keep out of their way. Factors which you must consider include:

- The visibility
- Number of other vessels in your vicinity
- Any limitation to your ability to manoeuvre, eg using a spinnaker in a sailing boat

If you have radar fitted you must not see this as a reason for allowing you to go faster because it is possible that your radar may not pick up very small boats.

3 Can recognise a potential collision situation

You must do all you can to check whether or not an approaching vessel is on a collision course with you. If you are in any doubt about the danger of collision with another vessel, take the greatest possible care.

The sure way to check whether or not there is a risk of collision with an approaching vessel is to take compass bearings of her. If there is no appreciable change in the bearing, she is on a collision course. If the other vessel is very large then take bearings of both ends. If her bows are drawing left and her stern is drawing right you are going to collide somewhere amidships.

If you do not carry a compass with which you can take bearings, you have to improvise. Check whether or not approaching vessels are moving relative to the background shore; if they are not, then there is a danger of collision.

If you keep a steady course and the relative bearing of an approaching vessel is steady you are going to collide. Be careful of this one, it is very difficult to judge relative bearings and it is also difficult to hold an absolutely steady course. This method of determining risk of collision can be useful only as a rough guide to approaching vessels which you have to keep a close eye on.

A rough guide to change of relative bearing – is the ferry moving against the shroud?

4 Can identify 'give-way' vessel in a collision situation

There are three parts to this section: sailing vessels meeting, power driven vessels meeting, and different sorts of vessels meeting.

There is also an overriding rule that in an overtaking situation, the overtaking vessel must keep clear (Fig 2).

There are just two rules to remember about sailing vessels meeting. If they have the wind on different sides, the one with the wind on her port side (the one on port tack) gives way to the one with the wind on her starboard side (the one on starboard tack) (Fig 3). If they both have the

wind on the same side, the windward boat gives way (Fig 4).

There are also just two rules about power driven vessels meeting. If they are meeting head on, both must turn to starboard so that they pass port to port (Fig 5). If they are crossing, the one that has the other on its

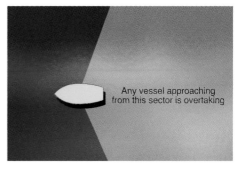

Any vessel approaching from this sector is overtaking

Fig 2 *The overtaking sector*

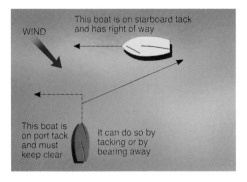

Fig 3 Port and starboard

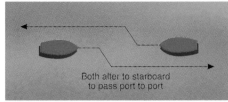

Fig 5 Power driven craft meeting head on

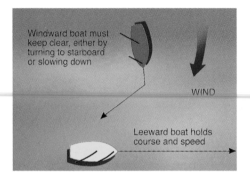

Fig 4 Windward and leeward

Fig 6 Power driven craft crossing

starboard side must give way (Fig 6).

When boats of different sorts meet, the general principle is that the more manoeuvrable must give way to the less manoeuvrable. In the following list each type of vessel must give way to any below them in the list:

- A power driven vessel
- A sailing vessel
- A vessel engaged in fishing (fishing does not include trolling with hand lines)
- A vessel not under command

or restricted in her ability to manoeuvre

Additionally, you should avoid impeding a large vessel which is following a narrow channel.

5 Knows what action to take as 'give-way' and 'stand-on' vessel

When you are the give-way vessel you must take early and positive action to keep out of the way.

Alterations of course are generally better than changes of speed because they are more immediately obvious to the vessel you are keeping clear of. The best possible manoeuvre is one which presents your boat at a completely different aspect when looked at from the vessel to which you are giving way (Fig 7). The manoeuvre to avoid is a series of small changes of course or speed because the other vessel is unlikely to notice that you are trying to avoid him and will be worried that you haven't seen him or are unaware that you have to get out of his way.

In a complex situation, in which there are several vessels converging or there is a lack of room to manoeuvre, the best action is sometimes to slow right down or stop.

When you are approaching another vessel and he has to give way to you, you should hold a steady course and speed. However, this does not mean that you should commit suicide by pressing on regardless of an approaching supertanker. If you are the stand-on vessel and you are concerned that the give-way vessel is not taking sufficient action to keep out of your way, you should take action to avoid a collision.

The only manoeuvre to avoid when you are the stand-on vessel is a turn to port in an attempt to keep clear of a vessel approaching from your port side. The reason is that if she makes a late alteration to starboard, which is the standard collision avoidance manoeuvre, just as you

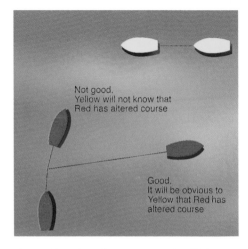

Fig 7 *Good and not so good collision avoidance manoeuvres*

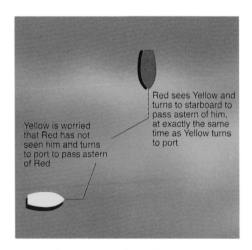

Fig 8 *The danger of an alteration to port to avoid a vessel closing from your port side*

5

start your turn to port you will turn directly towards each other, with disastrous results (Fig 8).

6 Knows the responsibilities of a small vessel in a narrow channel

When you are navigating in a narrow channel, you must keep to the starboard side of it.

In a small boat, under 20m in length, or a sailing vessel, you must not impede a larger vessel which is too deep to navigate outside the limits of a channel.

You must not cross a narrow channel if in doing so you would impede the passage of a vessel following the channel. Wait until she has passed and then cross.

7 Can recognise manoeuvring signals (1,2,3 and 5 short blasts)

The meanings of these signals, sounded on a ship's whistle or siren, are:

1 short blast: I am turning to starboard (1 is an odd number; starboard has an odd number of letters)
2 short blasts: I am turning to port (2 is an even number; port has an even number of letters)
3 short blasts: My engines are going astern (It doesn't necessarily mean that the ship making the signal is going backwards, but if she leaves her engines going astern she soon will be.)
5 or more short blasts: I do not

understand your intentions, or I do not think you are taking sufficient action to avoid a collision.

The sound signals may be accompanied by identical light signals.

8 Can make and recognise visual distress signals

Visual distress signals are little used nowadays but those with international recognition and likely to be seen are:

- A red rocket or hand flare or a red projectile flare
- An orange smoke signal
- Slowly and repeatedly raising and lowering arms outstretched to each side

Others which are still on the list but which, with every seagoing ship and most small boats nowadays carrying radios or mobile phones, are very unlikely to be used, are:

- A gun or other explosive signal fired at intervals of about a minute
- Continuous sounding of the ship's whistle or siren
- A signal consisting of the group ··· --- ··· (SOS) in the Morse code
- Code flag N over code flag C
- A square flag with a ball above or below it
- Flames in the vessel, as from a burning tar or oil barrel

See pp 7-8 for Self-test Questions on Regulations

Self-test Questions on Regulations

Try the following questions, which are typical of those asked about Regulations. Write down your answers and then check how you did against the answers on page 57.

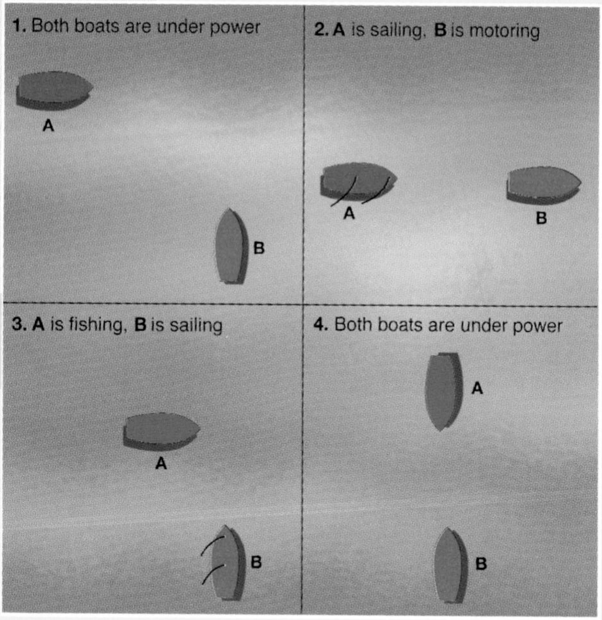

1. Both boats are under power

A

B

2. A is sailing, B is motoring

A   B

Self-test Questions: Part One

3. A is fishing, B is sailing

A

B

4. Both boats are under power

A

B

1 Under what circumstances would it be unnecessary to keep a good lookout in a small boat underway?

2 Name three criteria which you should take into account to determine a safe speed in a vessel not fitted with radar.

3 If you had no means of taking compass bearings, how might you judge whether or not an approaching vessel was on a collision course?

4 In the four diagrams, is **A** or **B** the give-way vessel (Fig 9)?

5 If you are the give-way vessel, would it be a good idea to make a small reduction in speed so that you pass astern of the vessel to which you have to give way?

Fig 9 Collision avoidance

6 When you are navigating along a narrow channel should you keep to the port or starboard side?

7 What is the meaning of two short blasts on the whistle or siren of a ship?

8 List three internationally recognised visual distress signals.

If you got all these right, move on to the next section.
If not, read the Regulations section again and try the following questions:

Self-test Questions on Regulations

Self-test Questions: Part Two

1 By what means should a lookout be kept?
2 If a boat is fitted with radar which is working efficiently, is it still necessary for it to slow down if it enters an area of fog?
3 What is the best way to judge whether or not an approaching vessel is on a collision course?
4 In the four diagrams in Fig 10 is **A** or **B** the give-way vessel?
5 As the stand-on vessel in a potential collision situation, what should you do?
6 You want to cross a narrow shipping channel but there is a ship approaching along it. What should you do?
7 What is the meaning of 5 short blasts on the whistle or siren of a ship?

8 Which of the following are internationally recognised distress signals?
   A An ensign hoisted upside down
   B A continuous sounding on a ship's siren
   C Orange smoke.

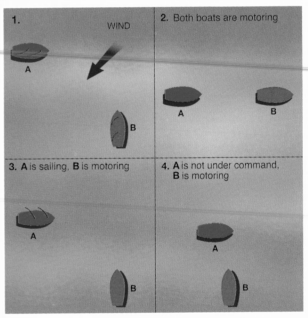

Fig 10 *Collision avoidance*

If you are still having some difficulty, move on to the next section, Safety, anyway and return to Regulations for another go later.

All Candidates: Safety

1 Is able to use and instruct crew on the use of

- Lifejackets
- Distress flares
- Fire extinguishers
- Kill cord (if fitted)

Lifejackets

You should be able to distinguish between a lifejacket and a buoyancy aid. The former is designed to support the wearer in the water with his or her mouth and nose clear of the water. The latter is designed to assist a person who can swim. A lifejacket has more buoyancy and it is distributed in such a way that it turns the wearer on his or her back.

There is an International Standard for lifejackets, and all lifejackets sold within the European Union must conform to the Standard. There are four levels in the Standard, each defined by the buoyancy, in Newtons, which it provides:

- **250 Newton Lifejacket** This is a very heavy duty lifejacket, intended for use by offshore workers wearing dry suits or other bulky protective clothing. It has a very large amount of buoyancy so that it can overcome any tendency for buoyancy from trapped air inside a dry suit to hold the wearer face down in the water.
- **150 Newton Lifejacket** This is the type in common use by yachtsmen sailing offshore.
- **100 Newton Lifejacket** This type is intended for use in boats which operate in sheltered waters, not far from rescue in the event of an emergency.
- **50 Newton Buoyancy Aid** This is used by dinghy sailors who need a flotation device which will give them some support in the water but which is not so bulky that it will restrict their mobility around the boat or catch on a low boom during a tack or gybe.

Children's sizes for each level of lifejacket are also available, manufactured to the same standards as the adult versions but they may provide less buoyancy because of the smaller size of body which they have to support.

An appropriate size of lifejacket or buoyancy aid must be available for everyone on board all boats. In open boats, without guardrails, a lifejacket or buoyancy aid should be worn at all times when the boat is under way. In larger boats the skipper should decide when the level of hazard is such that everyone should wear lifejackets. The choice between a lifejacket and a buoyancy aid must be made by the skipper of the boat who should decide whether absolute safety in the water or lack of restriction on board is the higher priority.

It is important that a lifejacket or buoyancy aid is the right size for the wearer and that the securing straps are adjusted to give a tight fit, otherwise the wearer may slip out of the lifejacket in the water.

Distress flares

There are four basic types of distress flare:

- **Red rocket parachute flares** These project a very bright flare high into the air. They are intended to have maximum visibility to raise the alarm in a distress situation. They are useless in very low cloud because the flare burns out while it is still above the cloud base. They should be fired pointing slightly downwind of the vertical because the rocket tends to turn into wind during its ascent. They must never be used close to rescue helicopters or aircraft.
- **Red hand flares** These are bright red flares which burn while held in the operator's hand. They are intended to pinpoint the position of a boat in distress. They should be held over the leeward side while they are burning so that any hot dross falls into

the water and not into the boat.
- **Orange smoke signals** These may be either relatively small and used in the same way as a hand flare; larger versions are thrown into the water once activated. Both types produce clouds of orange smoke and are particularly effective for indicating the position of a boat in distress in bright sunlight and to search and rescue aircraft.

The flares described above are virtually identical to those carried by merchant ships. The fourth type of flare is manufactured solely for the small boat market. They have a very short burn time, are less bright and can be less reliable.

All distress flares have a maximum storage life of three years and are marked with either the date of manufacture, the 'replace by' date, or both. Flares should be replaced by the end of their storage life.

Distress flares and all other distress signals must be used only if a boat or person is in grave and imminent danger and requires immediate assistance.

The firing mechanisms of distress flares vary from one manufacturer to another. Everyone on board, who might have to use a distress flare in an emergency, should be familiar with the method of operation of all the flares carried on board.

Fire extinguishers

Every boat with an inboard engine or a cooking stove should carry at least one fire extinguisher. In boats with living accommodation, the fire extinguishers should be mounted by the exits from the accommodation. In the event of a fire, everyone should evacuate the accommodation, taking the fire extinguishers as they go; once everyone is out in the open, the fire extinguishers can be used to attack the fire.

In boats with large inboard engines, there should be one or more extinguishers mounted in the engine space which can be activated manually from outside the engine space, or which operate automatically if the temperature in the engine space reaches a predetermined level.

Fire extinguishers for use in boats generally use dry powder as the extinguishing agent. If the extinguishers are left undisturbed for a long period of time, the powder can compact into a solid ball. These fire extinguishers should be removed from their mountings and shaken from time to time to keep the powder loose. They can be tested by rocking slowly while held close to the ear. You should be able to hear the powder flowing and there should be no clunking from a compacted mass of powder.

All extinguishers should be inspected from time to time to check that they all are in good condition and replaced if there are signs of corrosion.

Everyone on board should be familiar with the operating instructions for all the fire extinguishers carried.

The kill cord

The kill cord is a device on the end of a lanyard fitted to an outboard motor which must be in place for the engine to run. The other end is firmly secured to the helmsman. In the event of the helmsman going overboard, or falling off his seat, the kill cord becomes detached from the engine, which immediately stops. In small, fast motorboats, which can have a very violent motion when they hit waves or another boat's wash, the kill cord should always be attached to the helmsman.

2 Can prepare a boat for use and take sensible precautions before setting out, including:

- **Engine checks**
- **Check fuel for range/duration of trip**
- **Obtain weather forecast**
- **Avoid overloading boat**

Engine checks

The checks which need to be carried out will vary depending on the type and complexity of engine. For an outboard they might be:

Before starting Fuel in tank and cock turned on. Spare fuel in can, mixed to correct proportions if 2-stroke mixture. Lubricating oil level for oil-injection engines and 4-strokes. Spares on board, including a spark plug, spanner for changing it, emergency starting line, sheer pins. Propeller clear of obstruction.

11

Kill cord attached and secured to helmsman.

After starting Engine running smoothly. Cooling water circulating. Forward and reverse gears driving.

For an inboard diesel they might be:
Before starting Enough fuel for projected trip and fuel cock turned on. Fuel separator clear of water. Lubricating oil level correct in engine and gearbox. For fresh water cooled engine, header tank full. Cooling water strainer clear and sea cock open. Propeller clear of obstruction. Engine in neutral. Throttle operating freely. Battery switched on.
After starting and periodically while running Cooling water circulating and no excessive smoke from exhaust. Temperature and oil pressure within normal operating ranges.

Fuel and operating range or duration

You need to know the rate of fuel consumption for your engine at normal cruising speed and the capacity of the fuel tanks. It is then a relatively simple sum to decide what is the cruising range or maximum duration. You also have to decide on a sensible level of reserve fuel in case you need to make a diversion from your original plan or the weather worsens, cutting down on speed through the water.

For example, work out the cruising range of a small motor cruiser which has a tank capacity of 250 litres and cruises at 15 knots, consuming 20 litres per hour. The reserve fuel to allow could be 20% of total capacity which is 50 litres, leaving 200 litres of usable fuel. The running time available on a full tank would therefore be 200 litres divided by 20 litres per hour which is 10 hours; 10 hours multiplied by 15 sea miles per hour gives a range of 150 sea miles.

Obtaining weather forecasts

You need to know the common sources of weather forecasts and have an idea of their strengths and weaknesses.

The shipping forecast, broadcast by the BBC on Radio 4 Long Wave, 198 kHz, four times a day, gives comprehensive coverage of NW European sea areas and concentrates on features such as wind and visibility which are particularly important to boaters. However, each sea area is very large so there is no indication of local weather variations. There are equivalent forecasts provided by the national broadcasting services in most European countries, although many restrict the number of forecasts to two a day and most are in the language of the country from which they are broadcast.

Most television services include weather forecasts and have the advantage that the forecast is in pictorial form, so language is less of a barrier than with a purely spoken forecast.

In the UK, the Coastguard broadcast a forecast for local inshore waters on VHF marine band, every four hours. Again, most European countries have a similar type of service although few have such frequent updates.

Many marinas and harbour offices have a copy of the latest forecast displayed on a notice board, which is useful because it allows you to look at a forecast whenever you want to rather than just when the provider transmits it. Also available at any time are the telephone weather services, which provide recorded weather forecasts on premium rate phone numbers, and daily newspapers which provide forecasts, although they are, of necessity, based on yesterday's data. The internet is also a good source of forecasts.

Avoiding overloading the boat
Overloading is much more likely to be a problem with small than with large boats.

Every boat built or sold in Europe in the last few years has a plate which shows her principal dimensions, including her maximum carrying capacity.

Overloading small open boats gives rise to two types of danger. The first, which is the easiest to see, is a lack of freeboard. If the top of the boat is only a few centimetres clear of the water then the first wave or wash from a passing vessel will, at best, get everyone wet and at worst leave them swimming as the boat sinks beneath them. The other, more invidious problem of overloading is a loss of transverse stability. If you have too many people in a small boat, you raise the centre of gravity high above the level that the designer intended and she becomes very tippy. This may not immediately be apparent, until one of the occupants shifts his weight or stands up and the boat lurches onto her side, or even capsizes.

See p 14 for Self-test Questions on Safety

13

Self-test Questions on Safety

Once again, write down your answers and check with the answers given on page 58 to see how you got on. If you get all the Questions in Part One right, move on to the next section: CEVNI. If not, read the Safety section again and try Part Two.

Self-test Questions: Part One

1 In what type of boat is a buoyancy aid likely to be more appropriate than a lifejacket?
2 What type of distress flare would you use if you were in distress, quite close to other boats, on a very bright sunny day?
3 What in particular should you check about a dry powder fire extinguisher which has been in an unused boat for several months?
4 When should you use a kill cord?
5 What should you check in a boat with an inboard diesel before starting the engine to ensure that it does not immediately overheat?
6 You are going out for the afternoon in an outboard runabout. It carries 40 litres of fuel and uses 10 litres per hour at normal operating speed. How many hours of engine use do you have available with full fuel tanks?
7 What source of forecasts would you use to obtain inshore waters forecast in the UK?
8 If you were buying a new small sportsboat, how would you check that it was suitable for carrying the number of people that will usually go boating with you?

Self-test Questions: Part Two

1 Why is it important that all your crew have lifejackets which are a good fit?
2 What type of distress flare would you use if you were in distress far out at sea, with no other boats in sight?
3 How should the engine space of a boat with a large engine be protected against fire?
4 What is the purpose of a kill cord?
5 What do you need to do to the petrol for a 2-stroke outboard engine?
6 What is the range of a motor cruiser which has a 500 litre fuel tank, uses 40 litres an hour at normal cruising speed, and cruises at 18 knots, assuming that a 20% reserve is kept in hand?
7 Where might you obtain a weather forecast if you did not have access to a radio or television set?
8 Using a small boat which was not marked with a maximum carrying capacity, how would you judge whether or not you were overloading her?

If you are still having some difficulty, move on to the next section anyway and return to Safety for another go later.

B

Inland Only: CEVNI
(European Code for Inland Waterways)

CEVNI is the acronym for Code Européen des Voies de la Navigation Interieure. The English language edition is published under the title of CEVNI – the European code for inland waterways. CEVNI is a code for general conduct, markings, light and sound signals, buoyage, signs and rules of the road for European Inland Waterways. The regulations applied to inland waterways in most mainland European countries are based on CEVNI, usually with comparatively minor local modifications. The code is not, however, used on UK inland waterways.

Fortunately, CEVNI follows most of the conventions of the International Regulations for Preventing Collisions at Sea (IRPCS) and of the IALA buoyage system with which British boatowners are generally familiar.

A comprehensive summary of CEVNI is set out in *The RYA Book of EuroRegs for Inland Waterways* by Marian Martin, published by Adlard Coles Nautical.

For the sake of brevity, the following summary covers only those areas of CEVNI which are not duplicated in other international and UK codes and regulations and which are of significance to small pleasure boats. CEVNI contains a great many rules which are simply a statement of common sense, such as 'Vessels may not berth in sections of the waterway where berthing is generally prohibited (and 10 other obviously unsuitable places).' You are unlikely to be asked questions about these rules so no mention is made of them.

Rules of the Road

Small craft, defined as vessels under 20m in length, are generally required to give way to larger vessels.

In rivers, vessels proceeding upstream give way to vessels proceeding downstream. In general, vessels should keep to the starboard side of the channel. A vessel proceeding upstream which wishes to pass a downstream vessel starboard side-to shows a blue flag, blue board or a scintillating white light on her starboard side and she may also sound two short blasts. The downstream vessel indicates agreement by showing the same signal as the upstream vessel. This rule does not apply to small craft but it is helpful to understand it in order to anticipate the intentions of large vessels.

A vessel entering a narrow channel where the view is restricted sounds a long blast, repeated if necessary during the transit of the narrows.

An overtaking vessel should generally pass to port of a vessel which it is overtaking. An overtaking vessel may indicate its intentions by sounding two long blasts followed by two short blasts if it wishes to overtake to port; one short blast if it wishes to overtake to starboard. The vessel to be overtaken sounds one short blast if it is clear to be overtaken to port, two short blasts if it is clear to be overtaken to starboard.

A vessel about to carry out a manoeuvre, which will require others to keep clear, sounds a long blast, followed by a short blast if she intends to turn to starboard and two short blasts if she intends to turn to port.

Special signs are used to designate main and tributary waterways. Vessels entering and leaving harbours and tributary waterways in such a way that other vessels will have to manoeuvre to keep clear sound three long blasts followed by one short if turning to starboard, two short if turning to port, or just the three long blasts if they wish to cross the waterway.

Lights and day shapes

A vessel towing shows a yellow stern light instead of a white one. (IRPCS require a yellow and a white stern light so the difference is minimal.) A vessel under tow shows an all-round white light, or a yellow ball by day.

A vessel carrying dangerous cargo shows one, two or three all-round blue lights, depending on the nature of the dangerous cargo. By day the blue lights are replaced by blue cones, points down.

Ferries carry an all-round green light over an all-round white light or, if they have priority, three lights in a vertical line, green over green over white. By day a ferry shows a green ball or, if it has priority, a green ball over a white cylinder.

A vessel unable to manoeuvre (not under command in IRPCS-speak) may show a swinging red light or a swinging red flag or the two red lights or two black balls in a vertical line which is identical to the IRPCS signal.

A vessel having priority of passage shows a red pennant.

A stationary vessel at work shows two green lights in a vertical line on the side on which she is clear to pass and a red light on the side of any obstruction. By day, two green diamonds replace the green lights, a red ball the red light. If the vessel needs to be protected against wash, the green lights are replaced by a red over a white and the day signal becomes a red flag or board on the restricted side and a red over white horizontal striped flag or board on the side which is clear to pass.

Vessels of the supervisory authorities and the fire fighting services show an all-round blue flashing light. Vessels carrying out work on the waterway show an all-round yellow flashing light.

Waterway signs

There are five categories of signs:

- Prohibitory (Fig 11), which tell you what is forbidden (usually a red square and red diagonal)
- Mandatory (Fig 12), which tell you what you must do (usually red squares)

- Restrictive (Fig 13), which tell you what natural restrictions apply (again, red squares)
- Recommendatory (Fig 14), which give advice
- Informative (Fig 15), which tell you about available facilities and activities in the area (usually a blue background with a white picture)

Only the most common signs on which you are likely to be asked questions are illustrated here.

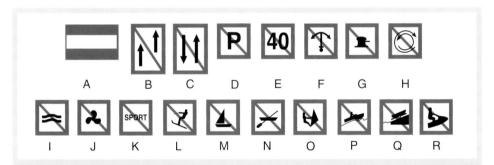

Fig 11 *Prohibitory signs*

A   No entry
B   No overtaking
C   No passing
D   No berthing
E   No berthing within 40m
F   No anchoring
G   No mooring to bank
H   No turning
I   Do not make wash

J   Motorised craft prohibited
K   No sport or pleasure craft
L   No water skiing
M   No sailing vessels
N   No manually propelled craft
O   No windsurfing
P   No speeding sportsboats
Q   No launching or beaching
R   No personal watercraft

17

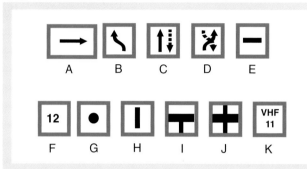

Fig 12 *Mandatory signs*

A Go in direction indicated
B Move to side of channel indicated
C Keep to side of channel indicated
D Cross channel as indicated
E Stop as prescribed in regulations
F Do not exceed speed indicated
   (12km/hr)

G Make a sound signal
H Keep particularly sharp lookout
I and J Do not cross main waterway
   unless clear to do so
K Keep listening watch on VHF
   channel indicated

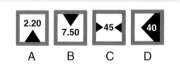

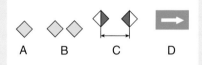

Fig 13 *Restrictive signs*

A Depth of water limited (to 2.2m)
B Headroom limited (to 7.5m)
C Width of channel limited (to 45m)
D The channel lies (45m) from the
   sign on the right bank

Fig 14 *Recommendatory signs*

A Recommended channel (in both
   directions)
B Recommended channel (in direction
   indicated)
C You are recommended to keep
   within the area indicated
D You are recommended to proceed
   in the direction shown by arrow

Fig 15 *Informative signs*

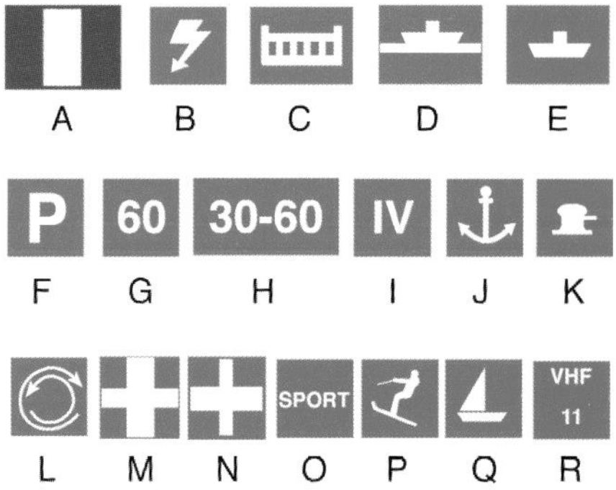
A
B
C
D
E
P
60
30-60
IV
F
G
H
I
J
K
SPORT
VHF
11
L
M
N
O
P
Q
R

- A Entry permitted
- B Overhead cable crossing
- C Weir
- D Ferry, not moving independently
- E Ferry, moving independently
- F Berthing permitted
- G Berthing permitted to a breadth of 60m
- H Berthing permitted at a breadth of 30m–60m
- I Maximum number of vessels to berth abreast is 4
- J Anchoring permitted
- K Making fast to bank permitted
- L Turning area
- M The waterway being approached is considered a tributary of this waterway
- N This waterway is considered to be a tributary of the waterway being approached
- O Sports or pleasure craft permitted
- P Water skiing permitted
- Q Sailing vessels permitted
- R Possibility of obtaining nautical information on VHF channel 11

Marking

Buoys and beacons conform fairly closely to the IALA system (see page 30) with a number of additions (Fig 16).

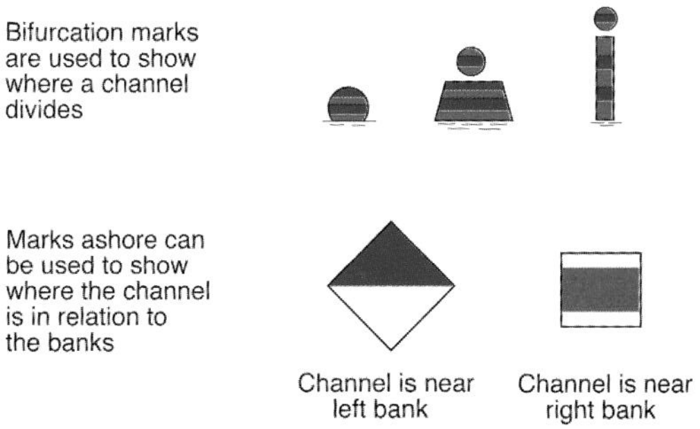
Bifurcation marks are used to show where a channel divides
Marks ashore can be used to show where the channel is in relation to the banks
Channel is near left bank
Channel is near right bank

Fig 16 *Non-IALA channel markers*

See pp 20-21 for Self-test Questions on CEVNI

Self-test Questions on CEVNI

As usual, write down your answers and check with the answers given on page 58 to see how you got on.

Self-test Questions: Part One

1 What is the meaning of one long blast on a vessel's whistle or siren?

2 What is the meaning of these lights on a vessel (Fig 17)?

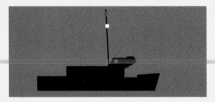

Fig 17

3 What is the meaning of this signal (Fig 18)?

Fig 18

4 What is the meaning of this signal (Fig 19)?

Fig 19

5 What is forbidden by the following signals (Fig 20)?

Fig 20   A   B   C

6 What does the following sign mean on a bridge over a waterway (Fig 21)?

Fig 21

7 What is the significance of a blue scintillating light on a vessel?

8 On which side would you pass a vessel showing this signal (Fig 22)?

Fig 22

Self-test Questions on CEVNI

If you got all the questions in Part One right, move on to the next section: Regulations. If you had difficulty with them you need to study *The RYA Book of EuroRegs for Inland Waterways* or the CEVNI section again and then try the following questions:

Self-test Questions: Part Two

1 What is the meaning of two long blasts followed by two short blasts on a vessel's whistle or siren?

2 What is the significance of a yellow ball displayed on a vessel?

3 What is the meaning of this signal displayed by a vessel (Fig 23)?

Fig 23

4 What is permitted by the signals in Fig 24?

A   B   C

Fig 24

5 What do the signs mean in Fig 25?

A   B

Fig 25

6 What is indicated by a blue board held out on the starboard side of a barge?

7 What is a vessel indicating by displaying a red over white flag?

8 What does this signal mean on a bridge (Fig 26)?

Fig 26

If you are still having problems with CEVNI questions, further study of *The RYA Book of EuroRegs* is needed. But take heart, the CEVNI test for an ICC also includes questions which you will be able to answer as long as you know the International Regulations for Preventing Collisions at Sea, and the questions are asked in multiple choice format, which most people find easier to answer.

C

Candidates for Coastal Waters: Regulations

We return to the International Regulations for Preventing Collisions at Sea, this time for the rules which cover Traffic Separation Schemes and lights shown by ships which you might commonly expect to see at night.

1 Knows the rules relating to Traffic Separation Schemes

Traffic Separation Schemes are the dual carriageways of the sea. Their limits are shown on nautical charts (Fig 27).

In a boat under 20m in length, or a sailing vessel, you do not have to use the separation lanes; you can use the inshore traffic zones instead and indeed that is a better place for small boats than in amongst the huge ships which use the lanes. If you do use the lanes you must follow them in the direction indicated on the chart.

You should, whenever possible, avoid crossing Traffic Separation

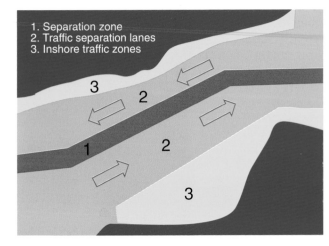

1. Separation zone
2. Traffic separation lanes
3. Inshore traffic zones

Fig 27
1 Separation zone
2 Traffic separation lanes
3 Inshore traffic zones

Schemes. If you have to cross one you should do so on a heading as nearly as possible at right angles to the direction of traffic flow in the lanes.

In a boat under 20m in length, or a sailing vessel, you should not impede the passage of a vessel which is following a traffic lane.

2 Knows the requirements for navigation lights and shapes to be displayed by own vessel

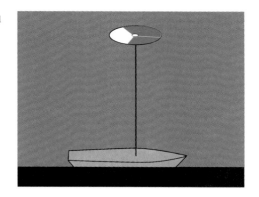

Fig 28 *Masthead tricolour light*

If you have a motorboat under 7m in length with a maximum speed of no more than 7 knots, the only light you are required to show at night is an all-round white light. If you have a sailing vessel under 7m in length you can have just a torch or lantern which you must show in sufficient time to prevent collision. (This gives rise to interesting speculation as to what happens when two small sailing vessels are merrily bobbing along on a moonless night waiting to shine their torches at anything which approaches.) However, both motor and sailing boats are asked to show the same lights as their larger sisters if it is practicable for them to do so.

In a sailing boat under 20m in length you have two options. You can either show, at the masthead, a tricolour light which shows red from right ahead to 22½° abaft the port beam, green from right ahead to 22½° abaft the starboard beam and white through the stern sector which is not

covered by the red and green lights (Fig 28). Alternatively, the red and green lights (described in the rules as sidelights) can be combined in a single lantern, mounted on the bow, with the white light in a separate lantern at the stern. The arcs of visibility of red, white and green are identical to those in the tricolour light (Fig 29). You can, if you wish, have the red and green lights as separate lanterns, mounted on each side, but this takes more power from the battery and is more likely to result in

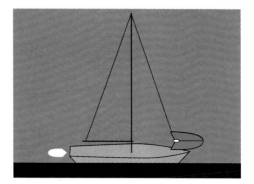

Fig 29 *Separate bicolour and sternlights*

23

the lights being masked by sails, so there is little point.

In sailing boats under 12m the coloured lights should be visible for 1 mile, the white light for 2. Over 12m, all the lights should be visible for 2 miles.

Powerboats under 20m show the same lights as a sailing boat, although they are not allowed to have them combined as a tricolour lantern at the masthead. In addition they must show a white light on the forward side of the mast (described, rather confusingly, in the rules as a masthead light) visible through the same arc as the red and green lights, ie from right ahead to 22½° abaft the beam on each side. The sternlight may be combined with the masthead light, so that it becomes an all-round white light (Fig 30).

In powerboats over 12m the masthead and sternlights may not be combined and the masthead light must be visible for 3 miles.

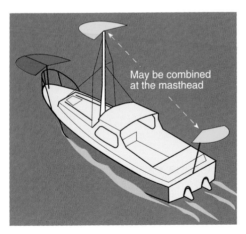

Fig 30 *Motorboat lights*

Sailing boats become motorboats as soon as they use their engines so a sailing boat has to have the motorboat lights available. When a sailing boat is motoring with sails hoisted it must show a black cone, point down (Fig 31).

Fig 31
Motor sailing cone

Boats at anchor at night must show an all-round white light. During the day they must show a black ball.

3 Can recognise the following from their lights:

- **Power driven and sailing vessel**
- **Vessel at anchor**
- **Tug and tow**
- **Dredger**

The lights for power driven and sailing vessels are easy, they are almost exactly the same as those described above. The main difference is that in a power driven vessel over 50m in length there has to be a second white masthead light, mounted aft of and above the first (Fig 32).

We have also covered vessels at anchor but more lights are required in larger vessels. Those over 50m must show an all-round white light at each end, the one at the bow higher than the one at the stern. Vessels over

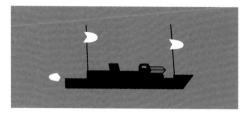

Fig 32 *Navigation lights for a power driven vessel over 50m*

100m are also asked to switch on any available deck working lights when at anchor. This certainly makes them easy to see but the working lights are often so bright that it is very difficult to pick out the anchor lights.

A vessel towing shows the same sidelights and sternlight as any other power driven vessel. Instead of the one or two masthead lights (depending on whether she is over or under 50m) she shows two masthead lights on her forward mast, in a vertical line

or, if the tow is over 200m in length, three masthead lights in a vertical line. Above her sternlight, she shows a yellow light, visible through the same arc as her sternlight. A vessel being towed shows just sidelights and a sternlight (Fig 33).

The rules provide for lights for two types of fishing vessels: trawlers and any type of fishing except trawling.

Trawlers show an all-round green light over an all-round white light. A trawler's fishing gear goes down into the water at a relatively steep angle so it is not surrounded by a lot of surface nets in which you could become entangled. Knowing this may help you to remember that her upper fishing light is green, indicating 'go' because there is no floating fishing gear to entangle you. (Trawlers do, however, behave unpredictably when hauling or shooting nets so do keep well clear of

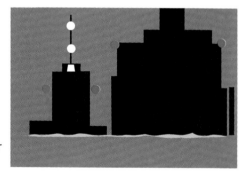

Fig 33 *Tug with a tow; overall length over 200m*

Tug and tow seen from abaft the beam

25

Fig 34 *A trawler's lights*

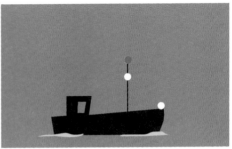

Fig 35 *A fishing vessel's lights*

them.) When making way through the water, a trawler also shows sidelights and a sternlight and she may also show a masthead light, aft of and above her fishing lights, although if she is under 50m in length she is not obliged to do so (Fig 34).

Fishing vessels other than trawlers show an all-round red light over an all-round white light. These vessels may have nets extending considerable distances from them along the surface, so the aide memoire is red for danger of entanglement in nets. If their outlying gear extends over 150m along the surface, they should show an additional white light, lower than the red over white, in the direction in which their fishing gear lies. As well as their fishing lights, these vessels show sidelights and a sternlight when making way through the water (Fig 35).

A dredger shows the normal lights for a vessel at anchor (or the normal lights for a power driven vessel if she is moving through the water while dredging) and in addition three all-round lights in a vertical line on her mast, red over white over red. If her gear causes an obstruction she shows two all-round red lights in a vertical line on the side of the obstruction and two all-round green lights in a vertical line on the side on which she is clear to pass (Fig 36).

Don't try to remember the exact detail of the lights which different types of vessel have to show; you don't need to be able to quote them. All you need to do is recognise a particular type of vessel from a picture of her lights, which is very much easier to do.

Fig 36 *A dredger's lights*

4 Knows sound signals to be made by vessels in section 3 above

This section refers to sound signals to be made in restricted visibility.

A power driven vessel under way and moving through the water sounds one long blast at intervals not exceeding two minutes. If she is not moving through the water she changes from one long blast to two long blasts. Almost every other type of vessel under way makes one long followed by two short blasts at intervals not exceeding two minutes. The exception is a vessel under tow which sounds one long followed by three short blasts (if practicable, immediately following the one long and two short blasts of her tug).

A vessel at anchor rings a bell for five seconds at intervals not exceeding one minute. If she is over 100m long she rings the bell forward and follows this by 5 seconds sounding of a gong positioned aft. An anchored vessel may also sound one short blast, one long blast and one short blast to warn an approaching vessel of her presence.

Vessels under 12m in length are not bound to sound the signals for vessels of their type but if they do not, they should make some efficient sound signal every two minutes.

See pp 28–29 for Self-test Questions for Coastal Waters: Regulations

Self-test Questions for Coastal Waters: Regulations

As usual, write down the answers and then go to the answers given on page 58 to see how you did.

Self-test Questions: Part One

1 If you have to cross a Traffic Separation Scheme, how should you do so?
2 What lights should you show in a 14m powerboat at night?
3 What lights should you show in a 10m yacht at anchor?

4 What type of vessel is indicated by each of the following groups of lights (Fig 37), and are you seeing her from ahead, her port side, her starboard side, or astern?
5 What type of vessel makes a sound signal in fog of one long blast at intervals of no more than two minutes?

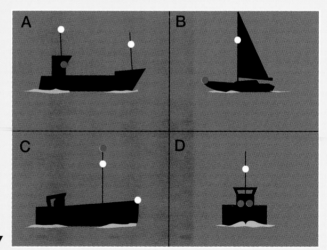

Fig 37

Self-test Questions for Coastal Waters: Regulations

If you got all the questions in Part One right, move on to the next section: Pilotage. If not, read the Regulations for Coastal Waters section again and try these questions:

Self-test Questions: Part Two

1 Are small vessels permitted to use the inshore traffic zones adjacent to Traffic Separation Schemes rather than using the traffic lanes?

2 What lights should you show in a 10m sailing boat at night?

3 What light should you show in a 6m motorboat with a maximum speed of 6 knots at night?

4 What type of vessel is indicated by each of the following groups of lights and are you seeing her from ahead, her port side, her starboard side, or astern (Fig 38)?

5 What type of vessel makes a sound signal in fog of one long blast followed by two short blasts at intervals of no more than two minutes?

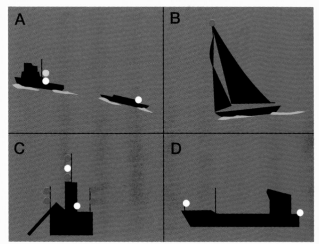

Fig 38

If you are still having some difficulty, move on anyway and return to this section later for another go.

C

Candidates for Coastal Waters: Pilotage

1 Can recognise, by day and night, and understand the significance of buoys of the IALA system

In the early 1970s, if you made a passage around Europe you were liable to encounter no less than 21 different buoyage systems. In the mid 1970s the International Association of Lighthouse Authorities (IALA) established a single system for use world-wide. There are actually two IALA regions: A which includes Europe and countries where there is traditional European influence, and B which includes North America and areas of American influence. There are differences between the way the IALA system is applied in the two areas, but for the purposes of the ICC test you only need to know about area A.

There are two families of buoys: the cardinals which are used to mark the side of the hazard on which they are placed, and laterals which are used to mark the sides of navigable channels.

Cardinal buoys

There is a certain logic about the colours of the buoys and the shapes of the topmarks. All the buoys in this group have a double-cone topmark. On a North cardinal they point upwards and North is conventionally at the top of a chart. On a South cardinal they point downwards and South is at the bottom of a chart. Now to a slight stretch of the imagination. On a West cardinal the double cones appear **W**asp **W**asted. On an **E**ast cardinal the appearance is **E**quatorially **E**nlarged.

The colours on these buoys are black and yellow horizontal bands. The positions of the points of the cones on the topmarks shows where you will find the black bands.

The lights shown by cardinal marks are even easier to remember because they more or less follow a simple clock code: the 3 and 9 quick flashes for east and west exactly mirror the positions of 3 and 9 on the clock face. The long flash on the end of south's 6 quick flashes is there simply to make it

Fig 39 *Cardinal buoys*

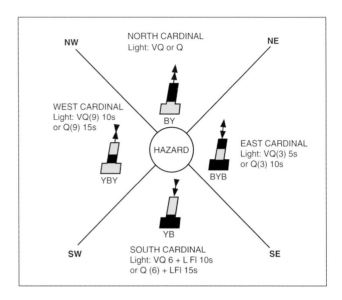

easier to distinguish from east and west when seen in a rough sea, but the 6 flashes conforms to the clock code. North's continuous quick flashing isn't an exact mirror of the 12 at the top of the clock face but having pinned down east, south and west the only place left for the quick flasher is north.

Lateral buoys

Red can-shaped buoys, or buoys with single red can-shaped top-marks, mark the port side of the channel, and green conical buoys, or buoys with single green conical top-marks, mark the starboard side (Fig 40). With a system which differentiates between the two sides of the channel there has to be a conventional direction of buoyage. Where the channel is the obvious route into or out of a harbour the buoyage direction is into the harbour, ie if

you are entering harbour leave red cans to port, green cones to starboard; if you are leaving harbour leave green cones to port, red cans to starboard. If lateral buoys are used in an area where there is no obvious route in or out of harbour the conventional direction of buoyage is clockwise round continental land masses. Where there is any

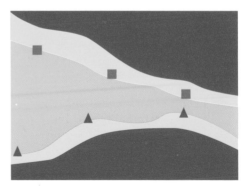

Fig 40 *Channel with lateral marks*

31

Fig 41 *Chart symbol for direction of buoyage*

Main channel to Starboard

Main channel to Port

Fig 42 *Bifurcation marks*

possible doubt about the direction of buoyage it is marked on the chart with a magenta arrow (Fig 41).

(Direction of buoyage is one area in which the seagoing convention seems, at first sight, to clash with the CEVNI convention for inland waterways. CEVNI defines the right bank of a river as the one on the right hand side of a vessel proceeding downstream. You then find that CEVNI uses red cans for the right hand side of a channel, green cones for the left. Think of a boat entering a river from seaward. Through tidal waters she will leave red marks to port, green to starboard. She passes

through a lock into the inland section of the river and she is now going upstream, leaving red marks to port and green to starboard. There is a sort of double negative difference between the conventions which has the effect of bringing them back into line with each other.)

The lights on lateral buoys could not be simpler, red lights on port hand marks, green on starboard.

Where a channel divides there can be a bifurcation mark which indicates which is the main and which the minor channel (Fig 42).

The colour yellow is used for marks which are of no navigational

Fig 42a

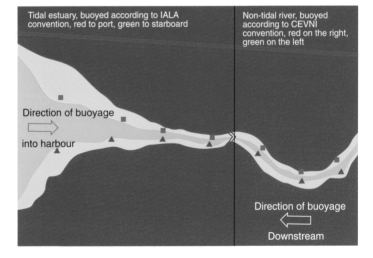

Tidal estuary, buoyed according to IALA convention, red to port, green to starboard

Non-tidal river, buoyed according to CEVNI convention, red on the right, green on the left

Direction of buoyage into harbour

Direction of buoyage Downstream

significance, such as racing marks and the marks which delineate a water ski area.

There are two other marks which are navigationally significant. The isolated danger mark is used only where it is possible to place the marker directly on top of the danger it is marking and hence it is more likely to be in the form of a beacon than a buoy (Fig 43).

Fig 43 *Isolated danger mark*

This mark, with its horizontal stripes, predominant use of the colour black and double topmark has much in common with the cardinal family of marks and you may find it easier to remember if you think of it as a centre cardinal mark.

The final buoy is the safe water mid-channel or fairway marker (Fig 44). This has much in common with the lateral series of buoys, including the single topmark, and it fits in naturally with them as a channel marker although in this case it marks the centre rather than one side of a channel.

Fig 44 *Fairway or mid-channel buoy*

2 Knows sources of information on:

- **Local regulations**
- **Port entry and departure signals**
- **VTS and Port Operations Radio**

This is a very simple section because it does not actually require you to know any facts, just where to find information. All the information listed will be found, in sufficient detail for the skipper of a small craft, in the yachtsman's almanac or sailing directions.

3 Can plan a harbour entry/departure, taking account of possible presence of large vessels and avoiding navigational hazards

When entering or leaving a busy commercial harbour it is important not to get in the way of commercial traffic. The first stage of planning the entry or departure is to study the chart and sailing directions, identify the main shipping routes and work out how to avoid them. In some ports there are channels or recommended routes for small craft, usually beside, but clear of, the main shipping channels. In others it is clear that there is sufficient depth of water outside the main shipping channels for small craft to use the buoys as a dividing line between the routes which larger ships must follow and the areas where the smaller boats can be reasonably certain of keeping out of the way.

Fig 45 *South end of the breakwater open north of the beacon clears the shoal. South end of the breakwater bearing no more than 110° (M) clears the rocks*

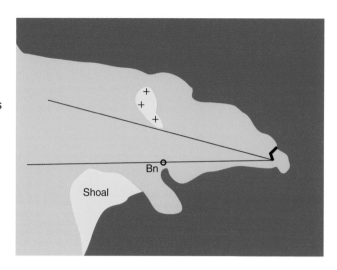

Inevitably there will be occasions when you have to cross the shipping channels to reach your destination. You should plan to do so at a narrow point in the channel, where you have a clear view along it in both directions and you should plan to cross at right angles to the line of the channel.

You should also plan to keep a listening watch on the Port Operations or Vessel Traffic Services (VTS) VHF radio channel. This is particularly important in poor visibility when, by monitoring the radio channel, you will hear ships requesting permission to leave their berths and reporting

arrival or expected arrival times at the port entry or at stages along the approach channel.

Avoiding navigational hazards in and around harbours requires a careful study of the chart and the tidal height for the time at which you expect to arrive or leave. You should then plan how you are going to avoid specific hazards, either by passing on the safe side of a buoy or beacon, following charted transit or leading line or just by keeping a careful watch on the echo sounder to check that you are not running into unexpectedly shallow water (Fig 45).

Self-test Questions for Coastal Waters: Pilotage

As usual, write down the answers and then go to the sample answers given on page 59 to see how you did. If you get all of these right, move on to the next section: Navigation. If not, read the Pilotage for Coastal Waters section again and try Part Two:

Self-test Questions: Part One

1 On which side would you leave each of the buoys or beacons in Fig 46 when entering harbour?

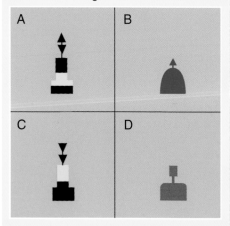

Fig 46

2 Where would you look for information on the local regulations for a harbour which you are planning to enter for the first time?

3 How would you plan to keep clear of the main shipping channel in a busy commercial port?

Self-test Questions: Part Two

1 On which side would you leave each of the buoys or beacons in Fig 47 when leaving harbour?

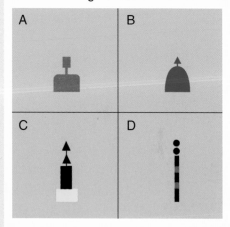

Fig 47

2 Where would you look for the channel number of the Port Operations VHF radio channel for an unfamiliar harbour?

3 If it was necessary to cross the main shipping channel in a busy commercial harbour how would you plan to do so?

If you are still having some difficulty, move on anyway and return to this section later for another go.

Candidates for Coastal Waters: Navigation

1 Can interpret a navigational chart, understand the significance of charted depths and drying heights and identify charted hazards

The extract from the chart of the French coast at Saint-Quay-Portrieux (Fig 48) is a good example of the way in which colour and shading are used to distinguish between land, the area between high and low water which covers and uncovers with the tide, shallow water and deeper water. To the left of the extract is land, coloured yellow, with heights and contour lines shown above Mean High Water Springs (MHWS). Moving to the right there is a narrow band which covers and uncovers as the tide rises and falls. Underlined figures here indicate drying heights, in metres and tenths, above chart datum. Continuing to the right is an area of shallow water, coloured blue, where spot depths are shown, below

chart datum. Next comes another area which covers and uncovers with the tide, again with underlined figures showing drying heights. There are some features in this area which never cover and the height of these, shown as figures in brackets, are measured above MHWS. Another area of shallow water follows, then deeper water, coloured a lighter blue, and then white for the area of deepest water. The line marked A-A' on the chart is illustrated in elevation on the diagram below it.

There are several hundred different symbols in use to represent different charted features, many of them easy to understand because they are just pictures of a typical example of the feature which they represent. They are all illustrated in a booklet produced by the Hydrographic Department under the slightly anomalous reference number of chart 5011. The more important symbols for common hazards are shown in Fig 49.

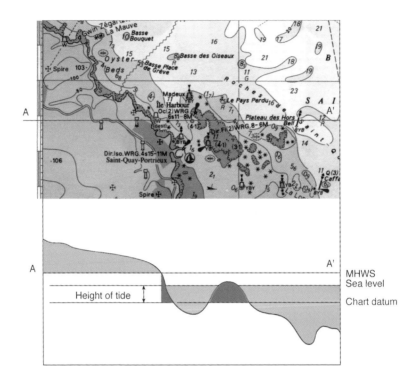

Fig 48 *An extract from a chart of the French coast at Saint-Quay-Portrieux*

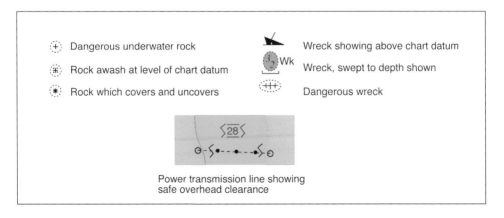

Fig 49 *Chart symbols for navigational hazards*

Under the title of the chart you will find some important information such as the scale and the units for depths and heights. Another important item of information for GPS satellite navigation system users is the horizontal datum to which the chart is referred. If your GPS receiver is not set to the same datum as the chart it could give you positions up to 200m in error.

Around the borders of the chart are the scales of latitude (on the sides) and longitude (on the top and bottom). Positions are often given in latitude and longitude, as degrees, minutes and decimals of a minute. The diagram shows how the latitude and longitude of a position can be referred to the scales (Fig 50).

The latitude scale also provides the distance scale, one minute of latitude represents one sea mile at that latitude. The reason why the scale is only valid at its own latitude is that on a Mercator projection, on which most small scale charts are drawn, the latitude scale is not constant but varies as you move north or south over the chart.

2 Can plot position by cross bearings and by latitude and longitude

Plotting a position by cross bearings is the usual method of establishing your position on the chart after taking bearings of three conspicuous objects ashore. Using three bearings is not necessarily any more accurate

than using two but it does guard against making a gross error, such as misidentifying one of the marks. Position A on the chart of the north coast of Jersey (Fig 51) is an example of a position plotted by cross bearings. The bearings which have been used are:

Grosnez Point	244°(T)
TV mast	175°(T)
3 masts	147°(T)

The bearings are then plotted using a patent plotter or parallel rule.

Position B is plotted by latitude and longitude and might have been taken from the readout of a GPS satellite navigator as:

49° 28′2N
005° 11′.8W

You can plot this position either with a plotter or a pair of dividers to measure off the northing and westing from the latitude and longitude scale.

3 Can determine magnetic course to steer, making allowance for leeway and tidal stream

This section requires an understanding of the difference between True and Magnetic courses and directions. The simplest way to deal with this is to think of True North as the direction towards the True North Pole and Magnetic North as the direction towards the Magnetic North Pole.

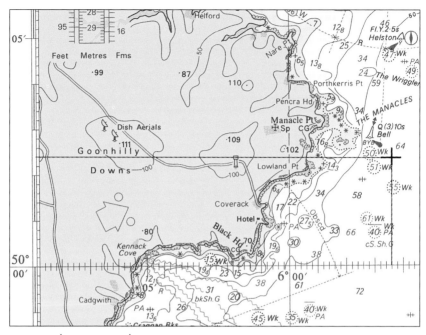

Fig 50 *The position shown is 50° 02'.4N 005°56'.4W*

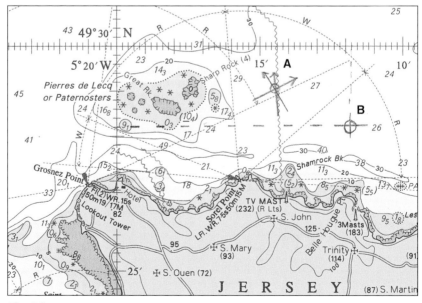

Fig 51

The difference between the two is the Variation, as shown below.

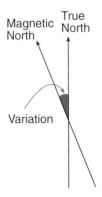

Variation is named East or West. It is East if the Magnetic Pole is to the East of the True Pole, West if the Magnetic Pole is to the West of the True Pole.

If you are using a patent plotter you can mark the variation on the scale and read off magnetic course direct, otherwise you have to convert between True and Magnetic following the rule:

To convert from True to Magnetic, add westerly and subtract easterly variation

To convert from Magnetic to True, add easterly and subtract westerly variation

Working out course to steer is done by drawing, and the best way to learn about the process is to take an example and follow it through (Fig 52). You are at S Trouvée buoy near the centre at the top of the chart extract, heading for the red and white fairway buoy in the bottom left corner. You are sailing at 6 knots in a moderate WNW wind, making 5° leeway. The tidal stream is setting east at 2 knots. Magnetic variation is 3°W. What is the magnetic course to steer, allowing for tidal stream and leeway?

For ease of reference, the departure point and destination have been labelled A and B respectively. The first move is to draw in a line representing the track you want to follow from A to B and to extend it some distance past B. Next, draw in a line, from A in the direction 090°(T), 2 miles long, to represent the distance which the tidal stream will move the boat in an hour. Label the end of this line C. Open your dividers to 6 miles, the distance that you will sail in an hour and, starting from C, mark off an arc across the line AB (or the extension past B of the line AB). Call this point D. Draw in the line CD and note the bearing, in this case 223°(T) or 226°(M). This is the course which you would need to steer if you were making no leeway. However you will be making 5° of leeway and to allow for this you need to aim off 5° upwind of the course you have just worked out, ie 228°(T) or 231°(M).

The most common error with this type of calculation is to join the end of the tidal vector, C, to the destination, B, instead of using the speed through the water and joining C to the line AB. The lengths of the three sides of the triangle ACD which we have drawn are proportional to the speed of the tidal stream (AC), the boat's speed through the water (CD) and the boat's speed over the ground (AD). We could just as easily have

40

Fig 52

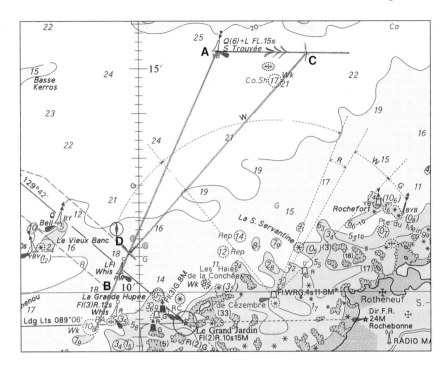

used 1 mile to represent the speed of the tide, 3 miles to represent the speed of the boat, and drawn a triangle which represented how far the tide would have flowed and the boat would have sailed in half an hour.

If this is not clear then have a look at the answers to the questions on Course to Steer at the end of this section.

4 Can use a tide table to find times and heights of high and low water at a standard port

Most tide tables adopt a layout which gives the tidal data for each day in a format such as:

16	0120	6.3
	0731	1.4
	1340	6.5
	1953	1.3

The first column with just one figure in it is the day of the month. The next column is the high and low water times and the final column is the high and low water height. In this example we are looking at the 16th of the month, there is a high water at 0120 with a height of 6.3 metres, a low water at 0731 with a high of 1.4 metres and so on. High waters and low waters are not actually named as such because it is obvious that the higher heights are high waters and the lower heights low waters.

5 Can determine direction and rate of tidal stream from a tidal stream atlas or tidal diamonds on a chart

Tidal stream atlases are available for most of the coasts of the UK and northern Europe. They consist of a page for each hour before and after high water, and high water itself, with arrows representing the direction of the tidal flow and numbers which give the rates at spring and neap tides, in tenths of a knot. For example the figures 08,17 indicate a rate of 0.8 knots at neaps, 1.7 knots at springs. Rates at tidal ranges between springs and neaps can be found by simple

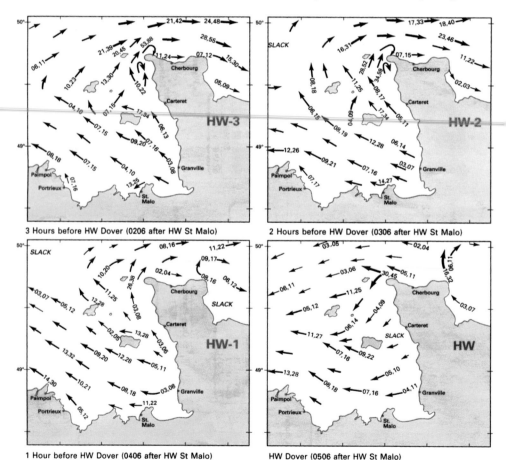

3 Hours before HW Dover (0206 after HW St Malo)

2 Hours before HW Dover (0306 after HW St Malo)

1 Hour before HW Dover (0406 after HW St Malo)

HW Dover (0506 after HW St Malo)

Fig 53 *Tidal stream atlas example. Courtesy of Macmillan Reeds Nautical Almanac*

proportion and there is a very useful diagram included in each tidal stream atlas which makes it easy to do this.

Yachtsmen's almanacs also contain tidal stream atlases, at a smaller size and in less detail than the full volumes (Fig 53).

Tidal diamonds on charts are another source of tidal stream infor-mation. The positions for which tidal stream information is given are shown as a magenta coloured capital letter inside a diamond. The direction that the stream is flowing and the rate of tidal stream in knots and tenths at springs and neaps is tabulat-ed for the hours before and after high water at a reference port.

See pp 44–46 for Self-test Questions for Coastal Waters: Navigation

Self-test Questions for Coastal Waters: Navigation

As usual, write down the answers and then go to the sample answers given on page 59 to see how you did.

Self-test Questions: Part One

Use the chart extract in Fig 55, on page 45, to answer questions 3 and 4.

1 On a green area of chart what do these figures mean: <u>4</u>3?

2 What do the chart symbols for hazards in Fig 54 mean?

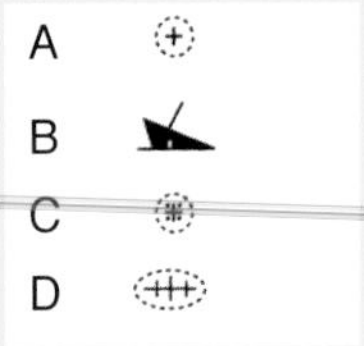

A ⊕

B ➤

C ⊛

D ⟨⊞⟩

Fig 54

3 On the sample chart in Fig 55, what is the latitude and longitude of the Plateau des Trois-Grunes west cardinal buoy (3½ miles northeast of Jersey)?

4 On the sample chart in Fig 55 you are in a motor cruiser at the centre of the compass rose and heading for the Banc du Chateau North Cardinal buoy (just over 2 miles east of Gorey on the east coast of Jersey) at 12 knots. The tidal stream is setting 020°(T) at 3 knots. Magnetic variation is 4°W and the boat is making no leeway. What is the magnetic course to steer? (If you find it too difficult to work accurately on such a small area of chart, write down the method you would use.)

5 In the following extract from a tide table, what is the time and height of the afternoon low water?

18

0211	1.5
0820	7.2
1435	1.3
2042	7.4

6 The rates on an arrow in a tidal stream atlas are shown as 06,12. What would be the rate in knots at spring tides?

If you got all of these right, move on to the next section: The Practical Test. If not, read the section on Navigation for Coastal Waters Candidates again and try the questions on page 46.

Self-test Questions for Coastal Waters: Navigation

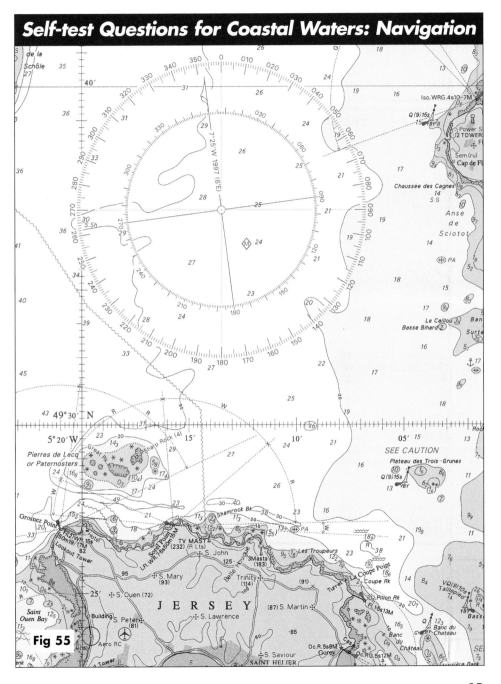

Fig 55

Self-test Questions for Coastal Waters: Navigation

Self-test Questions: Part Two

Use the chart extract in Fig 55, on page 45, to answer questions 3 and 4.

1 On a blue area of the chart, what do these figures mean: 6_4 ?

2 What are the meanings of the following chart symbols of navigational hazards (Fig 56)?

1   Wk

2   ⚹

3   ⬏

Fig 56   4   ⊕

3 From a boat north of Jersey, the following bearings are taken:

Grosnez Point	225°(T)
TV mast, 232m high	184°(T)
Turret at La Coupe Point	150°(T)

Plot the position of the fix. What is the nearest charted feature?

4 You are in a sailing boat at the centre of tidal diamond M (49°35′.35N 005°12′.30W) heading for the west cardinal buoy some 6½ miles to the northeast at 4.5 knots. The tidal stream is setting 340°(T) at 2.5 knots. The wind is north-westerly and you are making 5° leeway. What is the true course to steer? (If you cannot work with a plotting instrument and dividers on such a small extract of the chart, just write down the method you would use.)

5 To what level are tidal heights in a tide table referred?

6 If the rates given for the tidal stream at a tidal diamond are 2.4 at springs and 1.2 at neaps what will the rate be if the tides are half way between springs and neaps?

If you are still having some difficulty, move on anyway and return to this section later for another go.

The Practical Test

The practical session is an extremely important element of the test and the syllabus gives much more detail of what a candidate is expected to be able to do. The knowledge and ability needed to pass the written test is the same for all candidates. The practical test, however, can be carried out in the candidate's own boat, or a boat of similar type of the candidate's choice, so there is quite a widely differing range of skills required, to suit the type of boat in which you are taking the test.

As in the earlier section on the written test, the syllabus for the practical test is set out in **bold**; everything else is in plain type.

1 Start

- **Give safety briefing including use of safety equipment**
- **Has listened to weather forecasts**
- **Pre-start engine checks**
- **Start engine**
- **Check cooling**
- **Know fuel range**

All of this has been covered already in the written test; the practical simply confirms that you can actually do it in a real life situation.

2 Depart from pontoon

- **Understand use of springs to depart from lee wall/pontoon**
- **Communicate with crew**
- **Position fenders correctly**

Whenever possible, this part of the test is carried out with the wind blowing the boat onto the berth because this is one of the more testing conditions in which you might have to leave from alongside.

Whether you spring the bow off and motor out ahead or spring the stern out and leave stern first depends, obviously, on where there is sea room and also on whether there is any tidal stream or current flowing along the berth. In slack water, it is generally easier to spring the stern out and leave backwards because the shape of the bow of most boats makes it easier to swing the stern well clear of the berth before you leave. The stronger the wind, the further you need to swing the stern clear of the berth before you put the engine astern (Fig 57). If there is any stream

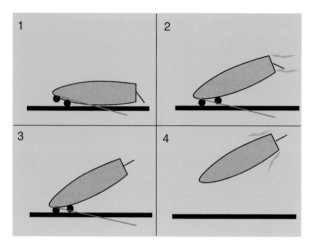

Fig 57 *Springing the boat out of a berth*
1 Let go all lines except headspring.
2 Motor ahead slowly, building up revs as necessary to swing stern well clear of berth.
3 Centre helm and put engine astern.
4 As the boat clears the berth, slip and recover the spring.

running along the berth then it will be easiest to swing the upstream end clear and the stream will help to lift the boat clear of the berth.

If you are asked to leave from the leeward side of a pontoon, don't make the mistake of rigging springs to swing one end out unless you have to do so to clear boats in an adjacent berth. Overcomplicating a simple situation is a recipe for disaster.

It is really helpful to your tester, as well as being good practice, for you to brief your crew on how you intend to carry out this, or any other, manoeuvre. In particular, it is good for everyone on board to know that you have foreseen any possible problems and that you have a plan for dealing with them. It is reassuring to the tester to know that the way you plan to carry out a manoeuvre is sensible. If he is uncertain about your plan, or fears that what you are about to attempt is doomed to failure, he is

going to be very nervous and the test will be much more difficult for you if he is hovering in the vicinity of the controls, ready to stop the test because he thinks you are about to attempt the impossible and do a lot of damage either to your boat or someone else's.

With any practical test, there is a tendency for the candidate to adopt the attitude that he must complete every manoeuvre which he is asked to perform, come hell or high water. This is unhelpful. There is always the possibility that the tester, who may not be totally familiar with the handling characteristics of your boat, will ask you to do something imprudent. If you think he has, say so and tell him why you think the manoeuvre is one which you would rather avoid.

It is also possible that you will be aware that a manoeuvre is starting to go wrong. At this stage it is vital that you remember that you are the

Fig 58a *How a boat turns: the paddle wheel effect. The prop turning anticlockwise pushes the stern to port. Think of the prop as the paddle of a paddle steamer and it is easy to predict which way it will operate.*

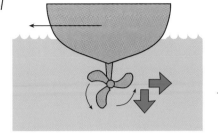

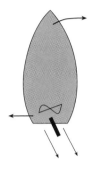

Fig 58b *The action of water on the rudder. The rudder deflects the water flow, either because the boat is moving ahead or because it is in the path of the slipstream from the propeller.*

skipper of a boat and not just a candidate in a necessarily slightly contrived test. If things are not going to plan, do what you would do in an ordinary manoeuvre; take the over-shoot, the safe option, and start again. You win many more points by showing that you can recognise a dangerous situation and avoid it than you do by pressing on and trusting to luck, even if luck turns out to be on your side.

3 360° turn in confined space

This is a manoeuvre which you may never have to carry out in the normal course of using your boat but it is a good test of how well you can control her. With twin screws it is a very simple manoeuvre, you just put the wheel hard over the way you want to turn, the outer engine ahead, the inner astern and adjust the throttles to stop

the boat gathering head or stern way.

With a single engine it is more difficult. With a shaft drive, the over-riding factor is usually going to be the paddle wheel effect: the tendency of the rotating propeller to drag the stern sideways. This is usually more marked when going astern than when going ahead so in a boat whose propeller drags the stern to starboard when going astern, it will be easier to make the turn to port.

One of the important points in this manoeuvre is that you should never allow the boat to gather any speed, ahead or astern. You can still use the engine to turn the boat by using short bursts of power with the rudder hard over. The slipstream from the propeller acts on the rudder to turn the boat before she gathers much headway. You then put the engine astern to kill any headway and impart just a little sternway. In some boats it is not worth reversing the

49

rudder because it has minimal effect when the boat is going slowly backwards but if you do, then make sure it is hard over in the direction of turn before giving another burst of power ahead. Effectively, it is the slipstream working on the rudder when the engine is ahead, and the paddle wheel effect when it is astern, that keep the boat turning (Fig 58).

The other factor which will affect the degree of difficulty of this manoeuvre is the strength of the wind. Most boats tend to 'seek the wind', whether they are going ahead or astern, and in some the effect is so pronounced, particularly when going astern, that the wind becomes an overriding force. If you have a beam wind at the start of the turn and your boat's wind-seeking tendency is more pronounced than her paddle wheel effect, then it will probably be easier to start by turning into the wind. If you slow right down before you start the turn, put the helm hard over and give a burst of power ahead, you should be able to turn the bow through the wind before you have to put the engine astern to stop the speed building up. If the space is so restricted that you cannot push the boat's bow past head-to-wind with the initial burst of power, then the manoeuvre may be impossible. The alternative of starting the turn downwind is unlikely to be any more successful; it will be possible to turn downwind, but thereafter any astern power will simply stop any further rotation.

With an outboard or outdrive boat, the manoeuvre is rather easier because you have directable thrust. It is just a matter of remembering to put full helm on in the required direction before giving alternate bursts of power, ahead and astern.

4 Securing to buoy

- **Communicate effectively with crew**
- **Prepare warp**
- **Choose correct angle of approach**
- **Control speed of approach**
- **Secure boat effectively**
- **Depart from the mooring safely**

If you keep your boat on a mooring buoy this part of the test should present few problems but if you seldom pick up a buoy, a little practice will be worthwhile.

To choose the correct angle of approach, look at the way that other boats on buoys in the vicinity (if there are any) are lying; the best angle of approach will be parallel with them. If there are no other moored boats around and there is any tidal stream running, the best angle of approach will probably be into the stream. The reason is that you will still have some steerage way even when the boat has stopped moving over the ground.

The other thing to look for is whether other moored boats in the vicinity are actually sailing over their moorings with a stern wind, so that the buoy rope leads aft from the stemhead to the buoy. Or are they lying back hard with their buoy ropes leading straight ahead and under firm load? This will tell you how difficult or easy it is going to be to stop when you arrive at the buoy.

However you judge the line of approach, you will usually be heading into the stream as you pick up the buoy. If there is no stream running, the approach is usually best made upwind. If there are very strong winds, a direct downwind approach may make it easier to keep the boat under control; it will certainly be easier for the crew to work on deck.

It is seldom a good idea to try to pick up the buoy directly under the stemhead. For one thing, this is usually the highest part of the deck and, in small boats, it is a precarious place to work. For another, you will lose sight of the buoy long before it is within boat hook range of the crewman, so you will have to rely on his instructions to direct the final stage of the approach. If you try to approach so that the buoy is picked up at a point some way aft from the stem (on the side of the steering position or on the side of the throttle control if you steer by tiller or a central wheel) you will have the buoy in sight much longer and the crew will not have such a long way down to reach for it. Don't worry about the buoy not being directly under the stem; if you have approached from downstream there will be plenty of slack in the riser chain which will allow the crew to carry the buoy up

to the stem once they have hold of it.

You have to be aware of two aspects of speed as you approach the buoy. If you allow the speed through the water to fall too low it will be more difficult to maintain good directional control. Judging speed through the water is a simple matter of looking over the side to see how fast you are moving, and if you are going too slowly, you can tell whether you need a burst of power because the steering becomes sloppy and unresponsive.

Just as important as speed through the water, is speed over the ground. If you are stemming a fast stream you can actually start to go backwards over the ground while still moving ahead through the water and maintaining excellent control. The easiest way to judge rate of progress over the ground, particularly in the final stages of picking up a buoy, is to find a transit of two objects on your beam and see how fast they are moving relative to each other. The one that usually presents itself is the mast of a moored boat and the land behind it, which is excellent as long as the boat is not sheering about wildly on its mooring, when it can give a totally false impression of how fast you are moving.

The easiest mooring buoy to pick up is the one with a small pick-up buoy which can simply be lifted out of the water with a boat hook. The most difficult is the low-lying buoy with a very small securing eye. One way of dealing with this is to drop the bight of a warp right over it so that the warp

51

catches the chain and nips it between its two parts. This allows you to hold the buoy close alongside while you pass a line through the securing eye.

Before leaving a mooring you need to have a good look round to check the positions of other boats under way in the vicinity. If you are secured to the buoy with your own warp it will be helpful to rig a slip rope, so that a crewman does not have to hang over the side to struggle undoing knots in lines under tension. If you are simply slipping a pick-up buoy it will help the crew if you motor forward slightly to give them some slack to work with.

5 Man overboard

- **Observe MOB or instruct crew to do so**
- **Demonstrate correct direction and speed of approach**
- **Make suitable contact with MOB**

The essential elements to get right in this exercise are:

- Never lose visual contact with the casualty
- Don't hit him with a turning propeller
- Get back to him without undue delay.

In a large boat, if the helmsman sees someone go over the side he may be able to swing the stern, and hence the propeller, clear of the casualty by turning towards the side from which he fell, but to have any effect, the turn has to be immediate.

If you have enough people in the crew, ask one of them to point at the casualty and to do absolutely nothing else. The boat will be turning quickly to return to the person in the water; there will inevitably be an atmosphere of shock and hence there may be confusion. The head of someone in the water is a very small object to find if you lose sight of it while the boat is turning rapidly; it is difficult to work out where to start looking, and hence the reason for telling the lookout to keep pointing at the casualty.

To some extent, the direction of approach to the casualty is a matter of personal preference. The direction of the tidal stream will have no effect whatsoever as it will move both boat and casualty in the same direction and at the same speed. A head-to-wind approach keeps the boat from rolling and there is no leeway to estimate and allow for. A cross-wind approach, upwind of the casualty, has the merit that you can aim off, stop near the casualty and allow the boat to drift down to him with the engine stopped.

Control of speed on the final approach is very important. You *must not* use astern power to correct an overshoot when close to the casualty, or you risk turning him into mincemeat. If you find, at the last minute, that you are going too fast, it is better to risk hitting him, leaving the engine stopped; you may give him a sore head but, unless you are in a large boat in a rough sea, you are unlikely to kill him, which you almost certainly will do if you hit him with a fast-revving propeller.

Once alongside the casualty, the first priority is to secure him to the boat. Unless he is already wearing a safety harness the easiest way to do this is by passing a bowline over his head and shoulders. Your technique for getting him out of the water will depend on the size and layout of the boat; the important point is to have a plan worked out in advance. You can test the practicality of your plan by putting a small inflatable alongside, getting the heaviest member of your crew to lie in it and try to rescue him. If you are going to include the approach manoeuvre in the practice, put a pair of oars in the inflatable, just in case your approach turns out to be less successful than you hoped.

6a High speed manoeuvres (if appropriate)

- Use kill cord if appropriate
- Choose suitable area
- Show awareness of other water users
- Warn crew before each manoeuvre
- Look round before S and U turns
- Control speed on U turns
- Emergency stop

This part of the test applies only if you are taking it in a planing motorboat. What you have to demonstrate is that when you use your boat's speed, you are aware of the danger and nuisance that you could unwittingly cause to others if you behave thoughtlessly. That said, the syllabus for this part of the test speaks for itself.

Your tester will be watching to see that you keep a really good lookout, that you are aware of what is happening all around you, and that you do not concentrate solely on the patch of water directly ahead. Most of the bad accidents involving planing boats, particularly the smaller and faster ones, are attributable to a failure to look around before a sharp high speed turn.

6b Handling under sail (if appropriate)

- Sail a triangular course with one leg to windward
- Choose suitable area for hoisting/lowering sails
- Use sails suitable for prevailing conditions
- Show awareness of wind direction
- Trim sails correctly on each point of sailing
- Warn crew before making manoeuvres
- Look round before tacking and gybing
- Control sails during tacking and gybing

As with the high speed manoeuvres, the syllabus for handling under sail is very specific as to what is expected of the candidate. Again, there is much

53

emphasis on thinking ahead and making sure that you have clear water before you start any manoeuvre. For instance, if you are hoisting or lowering sail while under engine, it is helpful to have a clear stretch of water to windward so that you can motor slowly with the wind on one bow while the operation is carried out.

If you are unfortunate to have chosen a windy day to take the test, it is sensible to err on the side of caution when deciding on the sails to set. It will be easy enough to shake out a reef in the main or unroll a little more headsail if you have overdone it but you won't look good if you lose control and round up in a heavy gust before you realise that you have too much sail set.

If you are sailing with a regular crew of many years' standing, you may well have come to know each other so well that you can sail in almost complete silence, giving very little warning or explanation before carrying out a manoeuvre. A crew that can work this way is a joy to watch but in the situation of an ICC test, the tester may wonder whether the skipper is really in charge or if he is being led by the crew. It is therefore advisable to be a little more talkative than usual. You need to show the tester that you really do know what you are doing (but do beware of overacting; you want an ICC, not an Oscar).

7 Coming alongside windward pontoon

- **Communicate effectively with crew**
- **Show awareness of other water users**
- **Prepare warps/fenders**
- **Choose correct angle of approach**
- **Control speed of approach**
- **Stop boat in place required and secure to pontoon**
- **Stop engine**

As with the exercise in leaving a berth, the coming alongside exercise specifies the most awkward situation.

Preparation and good crew briefing, including the plan for making everything safe if things do not go according to plan, are important in this part of the test. The worst thing that could go wrong would be half the crew trying to secure their end of the boat while the skipper and the other half are trying to go round again.

In most berthing manoeuvres, speed is unnecessary; it is just a potential to do damage. Berthing in an offshore wind is the exception to this rule, you have to make a reasonably fast approach or the boat will make so much leeway that you will end up either missing the berth completely or turning more and more into wind so that you finish up bows on to the berth.

If there is no tidal stream running, the approach angle needs to be broad, aiming initially somewhere in the

Fig 59 *Berthing in an offshore wind. Approach at a broad angle, aiming astern of the berth. Leeway increases as the boat slows*

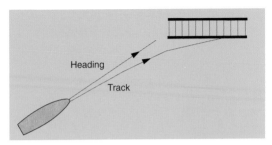

region of (or in a strong wind some way aft of) where the stern will be in the berth. Then, as you slow down and turn parallel with the berth, the leeway that you make will not matter, you will drift along the berth into the required position (Fig 59). If there is some stream that you can stem, this will help to counteract leeway and you can aim more directly for the berth. A downstream approach in an offshore wind is almost impossible; the combination of wind blowing you off and stream carrying you past, effectively prevent you from getting close enough to put a line ashore.

You are going to need some quick work from your crew to take lines ashore, forward and aft. The hand on the stern line needs to take it well forward, outside the guardrails, so that he can take it ashore long before the stern is anywhere near the berth. His job will be a great deal easier if he has the right amount of line to work with, a coil of spare warp is only going to complicate things and reduce his chances of getting the line secure in the short time available before the stern is blown off the pontoon. It is vital that anyone taking a line ashore

from anything but the lightest of boats takes a turn round a cleat and does not attempt to hold the weight of the boat himself. Once he has a turn round a cleat, he can control several tons with ease; if he tries to hold the line in hand he will be heading for a bad rope burn or a swim.

If you are going too fast as you arrive in the berth, make sure that the crewman on the head rope doesn't use it to stop the boat; he may well succeed but in the process the bow will come in very hard against the jetty or pontoon. Using the stern line as a brake will have less damaging consequences. The best tactic is a line from a midships cleat, which can be used to stop the boat without any damage, as long as the crewman surges the rope round the cleat to take the way off the boat gradually. If he tries to make fast immediately he may well part the line or pull a cleat out of the deck or the pontoon.

In a boat with high topsides it may be impossible, or dangerous, to put anyone ashore with a line; in which case the alternative is to secure both ends of the lines, throw the bights onto the pontoon so that

55

they surround their cleats, and tighten in on one end of both. This works best with heavy lines and a slow pull is more likely to capture the cleat than a quick jerk.

In very strong winds, particularly in a lightly crewed boat, the only safe way into a leeward berth may be to approach directly head-to-wind and secure the head rope. You can then take the stern line ashore and heave the boat parallel to the berth.

For the practical test you have to make up your own self-test questions; just take your boat and crew out and practise the eight elements which make up the practical test. You can be reassured that there is no special 'RYA method' for any of them; the right one to use is the one that works best for you, your boat and crew.

Good luck.

Self-test Answers

Below are given the answers to the first set of questions in each section.

Regulations

1 None. You must keep a good lookout at all times.
2 Any three from:
- The visibility
- Number of vessels in your vicinity
- Any limitations on ability to manoeuvre
- Background shore lights
- Weather and sea conditions
- Width of channel and depth of water
3 By lining up the approaching vessel with a fixed point on own vessel, taking care to maintain a steady heading, or checking whether or not she is moving against the background of the shore.
4 1) **A**
   2) **A**
   3) **B**
   4) Both **A** and **B** should turn to starboard.
5 No, you should make a substantial alteration of course so that the other vessel can see that you are taking action to get out of the way.
6 To starboard.
7 I am turning to port.
8 Any three from:
- A red rocket or hand flare or a red projectile flare.
- An orange smoke signal.
- Slowly and repeatedly raising and lowering arms outstretched to each side.
- Gun or explosive signal at 1 minute intervals.
- Continuous sounding of whistle or siren.
- SOS in Morse code ($\cdots$ --- $\cdots$)
- Flag N over flag C.
- A square flag with a ball above or below it.
- Flames as from a burning oil or tar barrel.

See page 61 for answers to second set of questions.

57

Answers to Self-Test Questions: Part One

Safety

1 Sailing dinghy or any boat in which physical agility is important.
2 Orange smoke.
3 That the powder has not compacted into a solid lump.
4 When the helmsman in a small fast powerboat under way.
5 That the cooling water inlet sea cock is open and the strainer is clear.
6 Allow 20% reserve (8 litres), leaving 32 litres usable. Plan for just over 3 hours available.
7 Either local radio, television or marina or harbour office noticeboard. Forecasts also available on the internet.
8 Maximum carrying capacity should be shown on a prominent plate affixed by the builder.

See page 61 for answers to second set of questions.

Inland (CEVNI)

1 A vessel entering, or in transit through, a narrow channel.
2 A ferry under way.
3 A vessel carrying dangerous cargo.
4 A vessel with priority of passage.
5 A Water skiing.
  B Launching or beaching.
  C Anchoring.
6 Recommended channel (in direction indicated).
7 A vessel of the supervisory authorities

or the fire service.
8 Pass it on the side on which it is showing two green lights in a vertical line.

See pages 61–2 for answers to second set of questions.

Regulations for coastal waters candidates

1 On a heading as nearly as practical at right angles to the direction of traffic flow.
2 A white masthead light, visible from right ahead to 22½° abaft the beam on both sides, sidelights: red to port and green to starboard, visible from right ahead to 22½° on each side, a white sternlight visible from right astern to 22½° abaft the beam on both sides.
3 An all-round white light.
4 A A power driven vessel, probably over 50m in length, seen from her starboard side.
  B A power driven vessel, under 50m in length, seen from her port side.
  C A vessel engaged in fishing, other than trawling, with gear extending over 150m in the direction indicated by the lower white light.
  D A power driven vessel, under 50m in length, seen from right ahead.
5 A power driven vessel, under way and making way.

See page 62 for answers to second set of questions.

Answers to Self-test Questions: Part One

Pilotage

1 A Pass to the east of it.
B Leave it to starboard.
C Pass to the south of it.
D Leave it to port.
2 In the yachtsmen's nautical almanac or in the sailing directions.
3 If there is sufficient water, stay outside the buoyed channel, if not stay as close as possible to the edge of the buoyed channel. If there is a recommended channel for small craft, keep to it.

See page 62 for answers to second set of questions.

Navigation

1 A drying height of 4.3 metres above chart datum.
2 A Dangerous underwater rock.
B Wreck showing above chart datum.
C Rock awash at level of chart datum.
D Dangerous wreck.

3 49° 28'.25N 005° 04'.95W.
4 See Fig 60, page 60. The method is as follows. From the starting point, A, draw the line of the course required to the destination. Next lay off the tidal stream for 1 hour to give point B. From point B measure off 12 miles to where it cuts the required course line and name the intersection point C. Join B to C and that is the course to steer, 164° (T). Apply variation:

True course to steer   164° (T)
Variation   4° W
Magnetic course to steer 168°(M)

5 The afternoon low water is at 1435 (in the time zone of the tide table, a correction for summer time may be needed) and the height is 1.3 metres.
6 The rate of the tidal stream at springs would be 1.2 knots.

See pages 62–4 for answers to second set of questions.

Answers to Self-test Questions: Part One

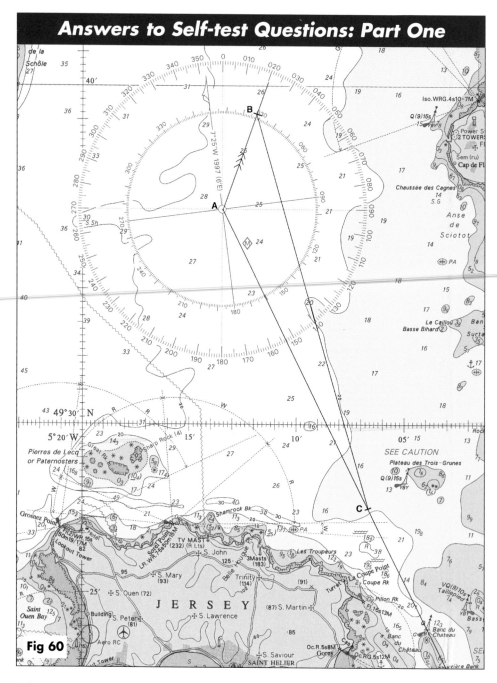

Fig 60

Answers to Self-test Questions: Part Two

Below are given the answers to the second set of questions in each section.

Regulations

1 You must keep a good lookout by sight, hearing and by radar if you have it fitted.

2 Yes. Radar may not detect small boats not fitted with efficient radar reflectors.

3 By taking a series of compass bearings. If the bearing does not change appreciably there is a risk of collision.

4 1) **A**
   2) **A**
   3) **B**
   4) **B**

5 Hold your course and speed, unless you are concerned that the other vessel is not taking sufficient avoiding action, in which case you should take action to avoid a collision.

6 Wait until the ship is clear and then cross.

7 I do not understand your intentions, or I do not think you are taking sufficient action to avoid a collision.

8 A is not. **B** and **C** are.

Safety

1 If the lifejackets are not a good fit it is possible that the wearers will slip out of them in the water.

2 A red rocket parachute flare.

3 It should be fitted with extinguisher(s) which can be operated from outside the engine space or which operate automatically if the temperature in the engine space reaches a predetermined level.

4 To cut the engine of a small fast boat if the helmsman falls overboard.

5 Add lubricating oil at the manufacturer's recommended ratio, unless it is an oil injection engine.

6 The reserve should be 100 litres, leaving 400 litres of usable fuel. This gives 10 hours at 18 knots, a range of 180 miles.

7 From newspapers, from a marina or harbour office or from a telephone weather service.

8 By checking that you have enough freeboard (height of side above the waterline) to prevent waves or wash from passing boats from coming on board. Also by checking that the boat does not feel excessively 'tippy'.

Inland (CEVNI)

1 I intend to overtake to port.

2 It is shown by a vessel under tow.

3 A ferry with priority.

4 A Sailing is permitted.
   B Mooring to the bank is permitted.
   C Anchoring is permitted.

Answers to Self-test Questions: Part Two

5 A Speed limit is 12 km/hr.
B Make a sound signal.
6 I wish to pass starboard side to.
7 It is clear to pass on this side but make no wash.
8 No entry.

Regulations for coastal waters candidates

1 Yes. They should use them in preference to the separation lanes.
2 Sidelights, red to port and green to starboard, visible from right ahead to 22½° abaft the beam on each side and a white sternlight, visible from right astern to 22½° abaft the beam on both sides. All three lights may be combined in a single tricolour lantern at the masthead.
3 You must show at least an all-round white light but if you can you should show a masthead light, sidelights and a sternlight.
4 A A tug and tow seen from astern (port quarter).
B A sailing vessel seen from the port side.
C A dredger, you are clear to pass to the right of her but not to the left.
D A vessel at anchor, seen from the port side.
5 Almost any vessel under way, other than a power driven vessel or a vessel under tow.

Pilotage

1 A To starboard (remember that you are leaving harbour).
B To port.
C Pass north of it.
D Either side but give it a wide berth, it is an isolated danger mark.
2 In the yachtsmen's nautical almanac or sailing directions.
3 Check for approaching ships, both by lookout and by listening on the Port Operations VHF channel for ships about to leave their berths. Try to cross without interfering with shipping movements and if possible cross where the channel is narrow and where you have a good view of it in both directions.

Navigation

1 Depth of water is 6.4 metres below chart datum.
2 1) A wreck, swept to a depth of 3.2 metres.
2) A rock awash at the level of chart datum.
3) A wreck showing above chart datum.
4) A dangerous underwater rock.
3 See Fig 61 for plotted fix. The nearest chart symbol is the 180° point on the compass rose.
4 See Fig 61. From the start point A draw the required course line

Answers to Self-test Questions: Part Two

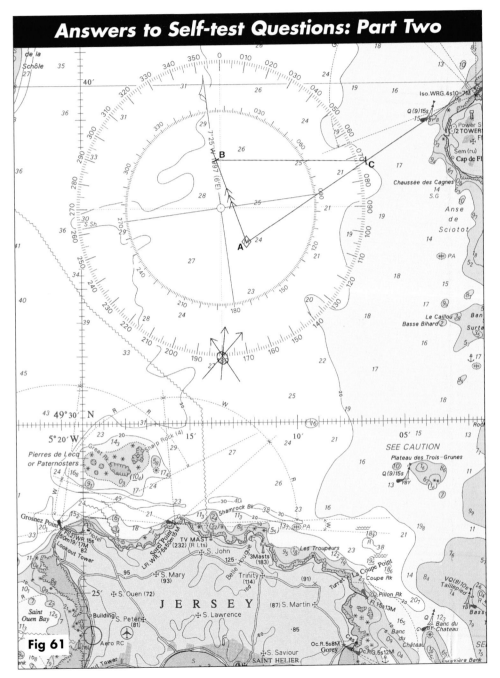

Fig 61

Answers to Self-test Questions: Part Two

through the destination. Draw the tidal set for one hour to give point B. From B strike an arc across the course line of 4.5 miles, the distance the boat will travel in an hour, and call the intersection point C. The direction BC is the course to be

made good, 090° (T). The boat will be making 5° leeway to starboard so you must allow for this by steering 5° to port, that is 085° (T).

5 Chart datum.

6 1.8 knots (half way between the spring and neap rates).

Index

approaching a mooring buoy 50-51
avoiding navigational hazards 33-34

berthing in an offshore wind 55
bifurcation marks 32
buoyancy aids 9-10
buoys 30-35
buoys and beacons 17-19

cardinal buoys 30-31
CEVNI (European Code for Inland
  Waterways) 15-19
chart symbols 32, 37
charted depths 36-38
collision, situation recognising
  a 2-3
coming alongside a windward
  pontoon 54-55
course to steer 38
cross bearings 38

departing from pontoon 47-49
determining magnetic course 38
distress flares 10

engine checks 11-12

fenders, use of 47-48
fire extinguishers 10-11
fuel and operating range 12

give-way and stand-on vessel, action to
  take 4-5
give-way vessel, identifying in a collision
  situation 3-4

handling under sail 53-54
harbour entry or departure 33-34
heights of tide 41-42
high speed manoeuvres 53

IALA system 30-35
ICC exemptions xii
International Regulations for Preventing
  Collisions at Sea 2-6
isolated danger mark 33

kill cord 11

lateral buoys 31-32
latitude and longitude 38
leeway 38
lifejackets 9-10
light and day shapes 16-17
local regulations, knowledge of 33
lookout, keeping a proper 2

man overboard 52-53
mandatory signs 18
manoeuvring signals, recognising 6
marks 17-19

narrow channel, the responsibilities of a
small vessel 6
navigation 36-46
navigation lights and shapes 23-27
navigational hazards, avoiding 33-34
Newton lifejacket 9

overloading the boat 13
overtaking sector 3

picking up a mooring 50-51
pilotage 30-35
planning departure 33-34
plotting position 38
pontoon, coming alongside 54-55
Port Operations 34
power driven craft crossing 4
precautions before setting out 11-13

recommendatory signs 18
Regulations 2-8
restrictive signs 18
right of way 4
Rules of the Road 15-16

safe speed, determining 2
safety 9-14
securing to a buoy 50-52
separation zones 22
springing out of a berth 47, 48
standard ports 41
starting out 47
syllabus 1

tests xii
tidal streams 38, 42-43
tide tables 41
Traffic Separation Schemes 22
turning in a confined space 49-50

variation 40
Vessel Traffic Services (VTS) 34
visual distress signals, making and
recognising 6
VTS and Port Operation Radio 33

waterway signs 17
weather forecasts 12-13
windward and leeward right of way 4